Bibliographic information published by the German National Library:

The German National Library lists this publication in the National Bibliography; detailed bibliographic data are available on the Internet at http://dnb.dnb.de .

Imprint:

Copyright © 2017 GRIN Verlag, Open Publishing GmbH
Print and binding: Books on Demand GmbH, Norderstedt Germany
ISBN: 9783668461321

This book at GRIN:

http://www.grin.com/en/e-book/367029/healthcare-information-needs-of-the-visually-impaired-bridging-the-visual

Fissha SeyoumTeshome

Healthcare Information Needs of the Visually Impaired. Bridging the Visual Impairment Digital Disability Divide

GRIN Publishing

GRIN - Your knowledge has value

Since its foundation in 1998, GRIN has specialized in publishing academic texts by students, college teachers and other academics as e-book and printed book. The website www.grin.com is an ideal platform for presenting term papers, final papers, scientific essays, dissertations and specialist books.

Visit us on the internet:

http://www.grin.com/

http://www.facebook.com/grincom

http://www.twitter.com/grin_com

HEALTHCARE INFORMATION NEEDS OF THE VISUALLY IMPAIRED

BRIDGING THE VISUAL IMPAIRMENT DIGITAL DISABILITY DIVIDE

Master´s Thesis
in Information Systems Science

Author:
Fissha Seyoum Teshome

7.3.2017
University of Turku

ABSTRACT

X	Master´s thesis
	Licentiate´s thesis
	Doctor´s thesis

Subject	Information Systems Science	Date	07/03/17
Author(s)	Fissha Seyoum Teshome	Student number	
		Number of pages	73p. + appendices
Title	Healthcare Information Needs of the Visually Impaired: Bridging the Visual Impairment Digital Disability Divide		
Supervisor(s)	Professor Reima Suomi and M.Sc. Neeraj Sachdeva		

Abstract

The focus of this research is to develop an understanding of how visually impaired people face a digital disability divide. The scope of this research is limited to people with visual impairments who may or may not have access to technology. The research shows how to bridge the divide while exploring relevant topics that lead to the conception of feasible solutions. Further, it will contribute to the development of more socially inclusive healthcare information systems.

The research is supported by a thorough literature review of articles, journals, and research reports dealing with the major relevant topics.

A qualitative research method was used to identify and obtain an in-depth understanding of the healthcare information accessibility (HCIA) barriers that visually impaired people face, and the factors involved in the creation of these barriers. Moreover, a quantitative method was used to collect primary data, and a number of different analysis methods were used to produce results. This led to findings that were generalized to the larger population of the visually impaired.

The research shows that, despite the staggering advances in information and communication technology (ICT), the healthcare information needs of the visually impaired are not being met. However, it has also been discovered that the digital divide caused by visual impairment can be mitigated with intelligent design and the realization of information systems intended to fulfill the healthcare information needs of the visually impaired. A logical information system is needed that has a combination of input, back-end, and output assistive technologies with increased social inclusion and the capability to empower visually impaired people and help them access available healthcare information.

Key words	Visually Impaired People, Healthcare Information Accessibility, ICT, Incentives for Healthcare, Barries, Factors, Assistive Technologies, Alternative Formats

ACKNOWLEDGEMENT

With love and appreciation, the Author would like to thank, all who had participated in making this research a reality. I would like to extend my thanks to Prof. Reima Suomi and M.Sc. Neeraj Sachdeva who supervised the research and guided the Author throughout the thesis work with dedication; the University of Turku for providing the excellent educational platform and resources needed to accomplish the thesis tasks online; the Finnish and the Irish delegates who collaborated in the data collection features of the research; family and friends for their continuous support in all aspects of the Author's educational activities including this thesis; and finally, God and The Lord Jesus Christ, who have sustained the Author without cease in all dimensions of life as well as in this research.

Table of contents

List of charts

List of figures

List of tables

Abbreviations

AT	Assistive Technology
CISs	Clinical Information Systems
D3	Digital Disability Divide
DAISY	Digital Accessible Information System
EHRs	Electronic Health Records
EMRs	Electronic Medical Records
EU	European Union
FFVI	Finnish Federation of The Visually Impaired
HCI	Healthcare Information
HCIA	Healthcare Information Accessibility
HCID	Healthcare Information Digital Divide
HCIS	Healthcare Information Systems
ICCPR	International Covenant on Civil and Political Rights
ICD	International Classification of Diseases
ICT	Information and Communications Technology
IHCIA	Incentives for Healthcare Information Accessibility
ISs	Information Systems
OHCHR	Office of the High Commissioner for Human Rights
PHRs	Personal Health Records
RNIB	Royal National Institute of Blind
UN	United Nations
UN CRPD	United Nations Convention on The Rights of Persons with Disabilities
VID3	Visual Impairment Digital Disability Divide
VIP	Visually Impaired People
WHO	World Health Organization

1 INTRODUCTION

1.1 Research Background and Motivation

Healthcare information is vital for health promotion, health protection, and the prevention of diseases. Every second, there is a vast amount of patient information being created by the different clinical information systems (CISs) to assist the healthcare delivery process. These systems include electronic medical records (EMRs); electronic health records (EHRs); personal health records (PHRs); and ancillary systems such as laboratory, pharmacy, and radiology information systems (Jacob 2008; Gunter and Terry 2005; HealthIT.gov 2015).

Access to this healthcare information both by the patient and the healthcare professional is crucial for making informed healthcare decisions. This applies to different demographic and healthcare settings. Failure to address a patient's right to access their own healthcare information (HCI) or to health-related information would result in a healthcare information digital divide (HCID). A digital divide exists between information haves and have-nots (Bucy 2000) and is a term used to describe the disadvantages faced by those who are either unable to or do not wish to use information and communications technology (ICT) (Cullen 2001). It is also a phenomenon of a multidimensional nature (van Dijk 2002; van Dijk and Hacker 2003 as cited in Wei and Hindman 2011). Among the clients of healthcare systems globally, the visually impaired are often victims of insufficient healthcare provision (Beverley, Bath, and Barber 2007; Saulo, Walakira, and Darj 2011).

There are approximately 285 million visually impaired people (VIP) worldwide. Of these, 39 million are believed to be blind while 246 million have low vision (WHO 2016a). Further, the International Classification of Diseases (ICD) has identified four levels of visual impairment: normal vision, moderate visual impairment, severe visual impairment, and blindness. Moderate visual and severe visual impairment are categorized under low vision. Those with low vision or blindness are said to be visually impaired (ICD 2006 as cited in WHO 2016a).

The Finnish Federation of the Visually Impaired 2016 has reported that Finland has about 80,000 VIP of which 10,000 are blind and 70,000 are partially blind in different ways (FFVI 2016). In the Republic of Ireland, there are about 12,995 visually impaired people (Green et al. 2016). In the United Kingdom, nearly two million people live with sight loss, but only 360,000 are registered as blind or partially sighted with their local authorities (RNIB 2014a). By 2020, the WHO estimates a two-fold increase in the number of visually impaired people worldwide (WHO 2016a).

Despite advancements in ICT solutions, there is a lack of coherent information systems and arrangements intended to fulfill the needs of this significant portion of the global population. Since the creation of Article 19, the right to information has become a fundamental human right (ICCPR 1966 as cited in OHCHR 2016a). Additionally, the Convention on the Rights of Persons with Disabilities states that disabled people have the right to information on an equal basis with others and through all forms of communication of their choice (UN 2006). Therefore, individuals have the right to information that is timely, that is in an accessible format, and with a high degree of relevance and use.

Several studies reveal that visually impaired people in different parts of the world wish to have access to healthcare information for the promotion and protection of their health and the prevention of disease (Cupples, Hart, and Jackson 2012; Beverley, Bath, and Barber 2011; Beverley et al. 2007; Saulo et al. 2011; Holdings 2009). According to these studies, the vast majority of the visually impaired want their healthcare information to be in an accessible format. Meanwhile, researchers have identified visual impairment as a major source of a digital disability divide (D3), and this posing a barrier to healthcare provision, which implies health risks (Beverley et al. 2007; Sachdeva, Tuikka, Kimppa, and Suomi 2015; Saulo et al. 2011). In the context of ICT, a digital disability divide exists between those with impairments and those without. This divide has multiple dimensions such as access, accessibility, and use. Its effect can be analyzed both nationally and globally (Dobransky and Hargittai 2006 as cited in Sachdeva et al. 2015).

There are various studies that report the lack of national arrangements for supporting the visually impaired in their healthcare information access (Cupples et al. 2012; Beverley et al. 2011; Saulo et al. 2011; Holdings 2009; Frances, D'Andrea, and Siu 2015; Kumar and Sanaman 2015; Ando, Baglio, La Malfa, and Marletta 2011). Some have disclosed the lack of collaboration between healthcare providers, healthcare professionals, and visually impaired patients and have suggested closer liaison between these groups (Saulo et al. 2011; Holdings 2009).

The main motives for conducting this research relate to the existence of conventions and laws in an effort to ensure information access rights for visually impaired people. These various studies report the interest in participation among visually impaired people in the delivery of healthcare processes. The healthcare information needs of the visually impaired are still unfulfilled despite the staggering advances in ICT that are seen in today's world. Hence, there is room, willingness, and the opportunity to bridge the digital disability divide caused mainly by visual impairment (VID3). This is important since, as discussed earlier, this D3 is caused by visual impairment and poses a threat to the health of this group of individuals.

Consequently, social inclusion can be improved by enhancing healthcare information systems while bridging the digital disability divide for the visually impaired.

1.2 Research Focus and Scope

Earlier studies have covered the various causes of digital divide. Several decades of researches has identified factors affecting digital information access; these include: finance (i.e. economy and income), social, government policies, ethnicity, gender, education, geographic location, and age (Rice and Haythornthwaite 2006; Wilson, Wallin, and Reiser 2003; Bucy 2000; Hoffman, Novak, and Scholsser 2000; Jones, Johnson-Yale, Millermaier, and Perez 2009; Hindman 2000; Wei and Zhang 2008; Loges and Jung 2001). However, these factors are generic and do not specifically address the impact of disability on the digital divide. A number of studies have shown that these factors also overlap with the digital disability divide. Emphasis should be drawn to social (Zetterström 2012; Wahl, Fänge, Oswald, Gitlin, and Iwarsson 2009; Mavrou 2011); financial or economic (Verick 2004); educational (Li 2010); and technological (Sachdeva, Tuikka, and Suomi 2013) factors.

This research assumes that people with autism, chronic illness, hearing loss and deafness, intellectual disability, learning disability, memory loss, mental illness, physical disability, speech and language disorders, and visual impairment face a digital divide and that each can have its own D3 category. A study by Sachdeva et al. (2013; 2015) has provided a conceptual framework for analyzing the digital disability divide.

This research paper focus on one type of digital disability divide—the visual impairment digital disability divide (VID3). For this reason, the scope of the research is limited to the digital disability divide caused by visual impairment. The paper will use of the conceptual framework developed by Sachdeva et al. (2013; 2015) as an example for analyzing the VID3. Moreover, it will find the communication barriers causing the VID3 and the factors associated with its creation. This will be done in relation to access, accessibility, and the use of healthcare information in the context of ICT. Above all, this paper will communicate on how to bridge the digital divide by recommending feasible solutions.

1.2.1 Research purpose and goals

The purpose of the research is to study the visual impairment digital disability divide. The goals of the research are to improve healthcare information access, accessibility, and use by providing a means to bridge the visual impairment digital disability divide using ICT. The collective actions taken to pursue and achieve the main goals of the study are listed below:

- Understanding the major HCI access barriers and the factors associated and the nature of visual impairment itself and its impact on information accessibility.

- Identifying potential areas of the research and the knowledge gaps thereof and assessing relevant earlier studies on the problem areas together with the corresponding investigation required to address them.

- Carefully documenting previous studies to support and make clear the contrasting methodologies and findings of this study.

- Studying the best practices that aim to facilitate and arrange ICT support services for VIP in a number of European countries and the United States.

- Investigating existing IS that are designed to support VIP in the countries of interest in this research, namely the Unites States, Finland, the United Kingdom, Ireland, and France.

- Examining available assistive software and technologies for VIP.

- An insight investigation into healthcare information sources and accessible formats.

- Exploring legislation and policies on accessible healthcare information that favor VIP.

- Discovering information systems and strategies that suit the needs of VIP in the countries of interest.

- Studying the relationship between ICT advancements and the healthcare information needs of VIP and making comparison among countries of interest.

1.3 Research Structure

This research has eight major chapters. *Chapter 1*: This covers the background and motivation; focus and scope; and the structure of the thesis. This section includes the purpose and goals of the research and the actions taken to pursue it.

Chapter 2 Healthcare Information Access: This part of the thesis will help the reader to understand information access in the context of the provision of healthcare services for VIP. Furthermore, it explores the barriers to healthcare information accessibility (HCIA) and the factors involved in the creation of VID3. Most importantly, it covers each type of barriers, namely awareness, accessibility, and motivational barriers.

Chapter 3 Healthcare Information Needs of the Visually Impaired: This chapter covers visual impairment and the digital divide; assistive technologies for the visually impaired; healthcare information sources and accessible formats; and legislation and policies on disability rights and accessibility, information systems, and strategies that suit visually impaired people. The last two explore their respective topics in the United States, Finland, Ireland, the United Kingdom, and France.

Chapter 4 Research Process: This chapter covers the research methodology and describes the methods used to conduct the research. Furthermore, it describes the data collection aspects of the research, which includes the survey of VIP institutes in Europe and secondary data on ICTs. Finally, it covers the data analysis section, which has two sub-sections: descriptive analysis and inferential analysis.

Chapter 5 Results: This chapter covers the results from the descriptive analysis and the regression analysis. In the regression analysis, the results obtained are classified into three groups: the overall data analysis; Finland data analysis; and Ireland data analysis.

Chapter 6 Discussion: This section discusses the results obtained for the three different cases. In each case, it goes through a statistical procedure to test the null hypothesis. Additionally, it gives an insight into the possible relationship between ICT and HCIA.

Chapter 7 Conclusions: This chapter summarizes the findings. The reader should, however, understand that some of the concluding comments are temporary as the situation may change over the coming decade. Most importantly, this chapter will suggest a feasible solution on how to minimize the visual impairment digital disability divide.

Chapter 8 Recommendations: This final chapter proposes future studies that need to be carried out as the continuation of this study. The impact of technology on the HCI accessibility of visually impaired people is given particular emphasis. Moreover, it will give general suggestions on how to resolve issues of awareness, accessibility, and motivational barriers.

2 HEALTHCARE INFORMATION ACCESS

2.1 Types of Barriers

For the proper promotion and protection of health and prevention of diseases, access to healthcare information is decisive. It is vital to understand information access in the context of the provision of healthcare services for VIP. In addition to the visual impairment itself, there are other barriers to healthcare information access to consider. These include awareness, accessibility, and motivational barriers. Identifying and addressing the barriers and associated factors that affect access should help to minimize the VID3. The apotheosis of technology's design and production will be measured by its capacity to enable the widest variety of disabled users to perform their daily tasks with little or no help from outside parties.

2.2 Awareness Barriers

2.2.1 Patients' presumption

Due to the awareness barrier, VIP are unable to access healthcare information, making the healthcare delivery process difficult as a consequence. This barrier has multiple aspects, which include patients' presumption or prejudice; providers' stance; executives' apathy; and manufacturers' exclusiveness. The author of this paper is convinced that understanding the nature of these barriers is a crucial step that must be taken before any attempt is made to reduce the VID3 effect. The four major social, technological, financial or economic, and legal factors are present here. The reader can identify these factors in the topics of barriers while contributing to the creation of the barriers.

Studies have revealed that the prejudice that visually impaired people have about information access contributes to creating this barrier (Holdings 2009; Martire and Iversen 2015). VIP's mistaken perception that particular healthcare information does not exist serves as a barrier to its access. Although this notion is based on reasonable premises, this is not always the case. Studies in the UK have shown that the majority of visually impaired patients do not inquire whether healthcare information can be presented to them in an accessible format (Holdings 2009). As a result, they are not aware of the different accessible formats available and hence the healthcare information is inaccessible.

Another reason mentioned in the report is the fear that VIP have of being treated by providers and other staff as people needing special care. The findings by Sharby, Martire, and Iversen (2015) in the United States shows that the visually impaired patients assume healthcare professionals do not take them seriously and thus they are less interested in accepting recommendations or asking for more care. Social, technological, legal, and financial factors are among the factors that affect patients' presumption barrier (Holdings 2009; Verick 2004; Sachdeva et al. 2013).

To minimize the effect of the social factors on the degree of VIP awareness, it is vital to work on social innovation. Social innovation is important for increasing the awareness and acceptance of technology among the visually impaired. One possible way for social innovation to emerge is by solving social puzzles both at the individual and the community level (Sachdeva et al. 2015). Technology also affects the way VIP search for digital information and as a result makes their access to healthcare information hazardous. For example, the progress of web-based information towards dynamic and interactive design has increasingly excluded VIP, consequently decreasing their awareness. This is especially true for those using technologies such as screen readers, which face difficulties when dealing with Flash, JavaScript, and PDFs (Brophy and Craven 2007 as cited in Kumar et al. 2015).

Legal and policy issues also significantly affect awareness among VIP. There have been situations in which these people could demand healthcare information in an accessible format, but did not as they were not aware of their legal rights. The report by Holdings (2009) shows that nearly two-thirds of the visually impaired did not know of the existence of policies and legislation that were designed to protect their information access rights.

Financial or economic factors affect VIP healthcare information access. Unemployment is common among VIP, which greatly affects their financial independence. As a result, the majority are from a lower socio-economic class where the availability of ICT facilities is scarce. In such cases, VIP's negative presumption about accessible healthcare information is understandable.

Unemployment is largely responsible for their financial problems and therefore governments, social institutions, and relatives of VIP are expected to do their part to reduce this problem. A study by Verick (2004) shows the importance of reformation that aims at hiring more disabled people. After the reformation came into effect, there was an increase in employment of 24% from an approximate number of 45,305 disabled people between October 1999 and October 2002.

2.2.2 Providers' stance

Healthcare providers also generate a barrier unintentionally for a number of reasons. Practices such as relying on others (i.e. family members, carers, relatives, etc.) to assist VIP; the lack of special training on the healthcare information needs of the visually impaired; and the lack of awareness regarding organizational policies, processes, systems, and support intended to address the healthcare information needs of the visually impaired (Sharby et al. 2015; Holdings 2009).

Let alone these group of individuals, that are relying on parents, carers, and relatives to obtain information while assisting VIP, it has also become the norm when helping children (Wilson et al. 2003). It is almost unimaginable to help disabled people without the direct or indirect involvement of parents. A study by Mavrou (2011) suggests the importance of professionals working closely with parents to provide disabled people with supportive policies and procedures in using assistive technology (AT). Beverley et al. (2007) also emphasized the inevitable involvement of carers while identifying and addressing the social and healthcare information needs of VIP. However, this practice must be discouraged as it continuously forces the visually impaired to be dependent on others as they do not believe the information they need is available in an accessible format. It also encourages healthcare professionals to rely on carers when helping VIP.

To remove the awareness barrier, the lack of training among healthcare professionals involved in the healthcare needs of the visually impaired should be considered. Various sources suggests that professionals first need training that increases their awareness of the information needs of VIP (Beverley et al. 2007; Holdings 2009; Mavrou 2011). According to these sources, providers do not understand any of the special needs of the visually impaired since they do not ask them in what format they wish to have their healthcare information. Additionally, the report by Holdings (2009) explains that healthcare providers are not familiar with the guidelines, policies, processes, and systems that are designed to support the healthcare information needs of VIP. Thus, most of the healthcare professionals are not aware of the special needs of the visually impaired and the existence of accessible formats if they exist.

Nonetheless, there are insufficient organizational resources, facilities, guide-lines, and support systems. This consequently poses difficulties for healthcare professionals while performing their duties. For example, according to Schiemer and Proyer (2013), the absence of awareness among ministries or school administrations on the special needs of children with disabilities in Ethiopia and Thailand is the reason behind budget allocation problems. The scholars emphasized the need to leverage resources by creating awareness among teachers and parents about the needs of children with disabilities. As discussed in most of the studies, this awareness will help to implement ICT in an appropriate manner. There is lack of nationwide governmental incentives that force disability equity. Disability equity requires the allocation of resources, ICT infrastructures, and systems for disabled people without discrimination on the basis of abilities (Borg, Larsson, and Östergren 2011a; Yeo and Moore 2003; Borg, Lindström, and Larsson 2011b).

2.2.3 Executives' apathy

The planning, directing, and coordinating of healthcare services are the major roles of healthcare executives and managers. Further, healthcare information initiatives, such as granting equal healthcare information access for all, should be the concern of healthcare executives. Healthcare managers must be aware of their responsibility in promoting healthcare information access for people with disadvantages.

The planning phase of healthcare services should take patient diversity into account. This will help to achieve a system that incorporates all patients into different healthcare settings. Crawford et al. (2002) mentions the importance of involving patients in the planning and development processes of healthcare services. Involving VIP in the planning phase will help to avoid inadequate development. Failure to involve this group of individuals while planning and developing healthcare electronic systems will result in inefficient systems. Walsh and Antony (2007) showed the existence of inadequate electronic systems by managers, which were intended to support paper systems while attempting to increase patient safety and quality. The authors suggest the need for coordination between managers and clinicians to develop tangible and specific joint action plans.

The direction and coordination of healthcare services will follow once managers have paved the way for the planning phase. Managers need to have enthusiasm for enhancing visually impaired patients safety and quality of care. This can be supported by government incentives that aim to help and coordinate clinicians and managers in making informed decisions about the utilization of resources (McAuliffe 2014). Having the right policies, guidelines, and processes is also important for directing and coordinating healthcare services for VIP. A report by the British Medical Association (2007) has urged managers to make policies and procedures more flexible and to come up with adjustments for meeting the needs of disabled people (BMA 2007). Such actions can improve overall healthcare delivery processes and at the same time increases awareness among the visually impaired about available accessible formats.

Nonetheless, the above studies have reported that there is a lack of enthusiastic leadership and active incentives from the executives for enabling healthcare information access to the visually impaired, which creates the barrier. There is a need for a coordinated effort between healthcare professional and healthcare managers to work together. There is a positive outcome from the participation of VIP while developing a healthcare service. Healthcare managers should make transparent healthcare information delivery guidelines, policies, processes, and models available to healthcare professionals.

2.2.4 Manufacturers' exclusiveness

The exclusion of the visually impaired by manufacturers during device production is known to generate most of the problems in healthcare information access. The lack of awareness related to disability issues by device manufacturers has played a role in the mass production of technological devices that exclude VIP as consumers (Sachdeva et al. 2015). Manufacturers must re-evaluate their customer segment and come up with a production plan that includes the visually impaired. It is also relevant to demand the participation of VIP in the design process. Universal design implicitly suggests that the creation of devices, ICT environments, systems, and processes must take into account VIP abilities. Devices should be produced that increase their capabilities while working in different circumstances, conditions, and environments (Vanderheiden 1996 as cited in Kleynhans and Fourie 2014).

Smart devices such as mobile phones and tablets have the potential to give freedom to people with disabilities, including the group under discussion, to act independently (Kane, Jayant, Wobbrock, and Ladner 2009). Hence, these technologies can help them to access healthcare information by themselves while keeping in contact with families and caregivers. The problem is that mobile manufacturers are not considering people with disabilities and elderly people while mass producing mobile devices. The user interfaces are often unfriendly and inaccessible for people with visual and motor impairments (Dawe 2007 and Kurniawan 2008 as cited in Kane et al. 2009).

There have been attempts by manufacturers to address users with disabilities by producing special tools and devices such as VIP PAC Mate Accessible Note and the Mobile Speak screen reader. However, these are expensive and they are equipped with reduced features. Thus, the visually impaired is forced to use the mass produced general purpose devices, which have poor usability (Dawe 2007 as cited in Kane et al. 2009).

Therefore, exclusive mass production is a major problem that demands collaboration between governments, healthcare managers, healthcare professionals, and even VIP globally. Having the laws, standards, and regulations that address the information rights of this minority group is not enough. Instead, a pragmatic view of solving the problem must be conceived. One example that is already in practice is called Design for All (Kleynhans and Fourie 2014). Universal usability is the answer, but understanding users in the international market is still a challenge. Building a system using universal design (Design for All) will require the incorporation of user diversity, different types of technology, and gaps in user knowledge (Shneiderman et al. as cited in Jhangianti 2006).

2.3 Accessibility Barriers

The accessibility barriers refers to situations in which healthcare information becomes unavailable to the heterogeneous group of VIP due to social, technological, financial or economic, and legal factors. Technology plays an important role in increasing the accessibility of healthcare information to the visually impaired. It does this by enhancing the usability of devices, products, and services. As a result, technology creates a facilitated ICT environment for a wide range of people with different abilities. It can create properties within a product, service, or facility that can enable people with a wide range of capabilities (HFES 2008). For the visually impaired, there are a number of examples of accessibility barriers that are technical in origin. These include inaccessible information formats such as braille, images without text, inadequately described complex images, videos without text or audio, dynamically changing web content, and content logics that are only presented visually.

As long as it remains outside the legal reach of the VIP, it is not enough to know that the healthcare information is out there to be accessed. This brings us to the legal factors that contribute to the accessibility barrier. There are already laws and standards that are intended to defend the information rights of disabled people (ICCPR 1966 as cited in OHCHR 2016a; UN 2006). There is also a convention with detailed applicability guidelines (UN 2006). However, these are not properly enforced and has not been widely applied by governments, manufacturers, healthcare providers, and healthcare professionals. Studies have urged for more government incentives to enforce laws that have the potential to empower the visually impaired while reducing the D3 (Kelly and Clark-Bischke 2011; Cooper, Sloan, Kelly, and Lewthwaite 2012; Sloan and Phipps 2003 as cited in Sachdeva et al. 2015).

Purchasing power and accessibility are directly proportional for disabled people. The financial situations of VIP decide whether or not they can afford to buy assistive technologies (ATs) designed for them. On one hand, their financial capability is greatly affected by employment (Borg et al. 2011b). Being disabled will seriously affect the probability of being employed (Nyman et al. 2012 as cited in Coffey, Coufopoulos, and Kinghorn 2014). In their study, Vicente and Lopez (2010) showed that the majority of disabled people are in a lower socio-economic class. This is due to a lack of opportunities in terms of education and training, which consequently affects their income. Because of this they are less likely to make use of the Internet and other paid ICT facilities. Thus, social exclusion is increasing for these individuals, and their limited access to technology is intensifying the VID3 effect.

The social factor is cosmopolitan in its influence and significantly affects the visual impairment digital disability divide. Having the appropriate social healthcare infrastructure is vital for the visually impaired to increase the accessibility of HCI. Employment has a positive impact on social inclusion. Allowing the visually impaired to engage in social activities will help to devise ways to educate and train them and this will alleviate the unemployment problem. Hyde (1996), as cited in Coffey et al. (2014), shares similar thoughts about employment's capacity to increase income and enhance the quality of life and health while reducing social exclusion and poverty. Therefore, the effort to employ VIP will encourage social innovations that create ICT facilities in all sectors of social services including healthcare. At the same time, this will increase healthcare information accessibility (HCIA), which will result in the reduction of VID3.

2.4 Motivational Barriers

Motivational barriers exists due to the complex multidimensional interactions between social, financial, legal, and technological factors. From the earlier discussions, it is possible to deduce that these factors predominantly impact healthcare information availability to VIP positively or negatively. Furthermore, they have a tangible influence on the motivation of these people mainly in their attitude towards the use of technology. According to Sachdeva et al. (2015), an individual's motivational status is the result of three core features, namely attitude, education, and knowledge and skills. De Boeck et al. (2012), as cited in Sachdeva et al. (2015), explains the reason that VIP are reluctant to use assistive technologies. Predominantly, this is because of their negative attitude about the use of technology in the first place. However, after mentioning the negligible effect of attitude on the digital disability divide, the author placed an emphasis on providing opportunities.

Other scholars have also studied the attitudinal differences that the general public and the disabled people hold towards ICT (Vicente et al. 2010). According to Seniorwatch (2002) and Segrist (2004), as cited in Vicente et al. (2010), a great deal of attention is given to the lack of interest and motivation among elderly and disabled people towards ICT, which has contributed to the poor levels of access to the Internet. This is also the underlying reason for the rare usage of technology among disabled people.

The relation between education and motivation is worth studying to minimize VID3. There is a lack of enforcement of the laws that enable education and could create possibilities for employment, thus raising the quality of life in terms of income and access to healthcare services (Sachdeva et al. 2015). This is possible since education serves as a platform to gain the knowledge and skills necessary to be competent in the job market by minimizing the impact of an individual's disability. Studies by Schiemer et al. (2013) and Sachdeva et al. (2015) have shown that education can be facilitated by ICT, which implies that education and information and communication technologies are inseparable, each benefiting the other. Today, the means of communication between people for any purpose and under any field of study or activity are being increasingly facilitated by ICT. Education is no different and, even in developing nations, the use of the Internet and mobile devices is encouraged to benefit society while facilitating learning.

Education activates processes of giving and receiving intended-purpose instructions. These processes, which are forms of studies, are responsible for the acquisition of knowledge and skills. This is important for keeping an individual's motivation high enough to perform important tasks. Scholars have emphasized the importance of knowledge and skills to keep people with disabilities motivated to use technology (Schiemer et al. 2013; Victory and Cooper 2002; Fox and Livingston 2007 as cited in Sachdeva et al. 2015). Knowledge and skills about the use and application of information and communication technologies are highly recommended for parents and teachers who deal with disabled children. Schiemer et al. (2013) shares a similar thought, stating that having only superficial knowledge and skill about ICT will consume a great deal of a teacher's time when planning and preparing the classes.

Even in a scenario where all of these problems have been solved, motivational barriers will still exist. This is true with the omission of all the social, financial, and technological factors affecting the motivation of VIP and further exacerbating the VID3 effect. Motivational barriers can still emerge from the increase in digitization process, which creates vast amounts of healthcare information. Although this may be present in accessible formats or without duplication, it may be too easy to access too much content, making the visually impaired less zealous. This implies the need for an intrinsic motivation from all visually impaired people to remove completely the VID3; nonetheless, this is only theoretical. Figure 1 summarizes the relationship between the barriers to healthcare information access and the factors involved in their creation.

Figure 1: The relationship between the barriers to healthcare information access and the factors involved in their creation.

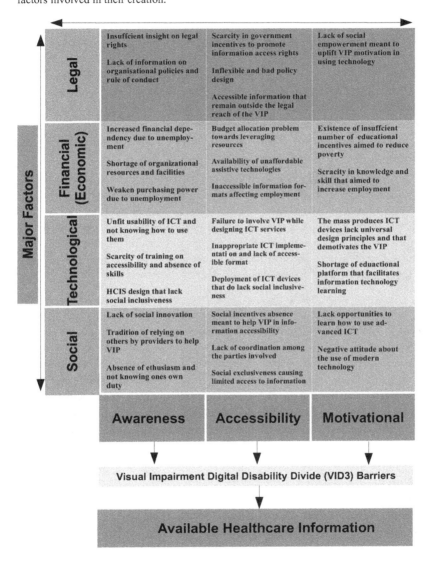

Source: The author's work, based on the conceptual framework developed by Sachdeva et al. (2013; 2015).

3 HEALTHCARE INFORMATION NEEDS OF THE VISUALLY IMPAIRED

3.1 Visual Impairment and the Digital Divide

A visual impairment is "any degree of vision loss that affects an individual's ability to perform daily life tasks, caused by a visual system that is not working properly or not formed correctly" (Corn and Koenig 1995, 452 as cited in Sapp 2003). It is marked by the weakening of an individual's visual capability as a result of disease, trauma, congenital, and degenerative conditions that are incurable by refractive correction, medication, or surgery (Pal, Pradhan, Shah, and Babu 2011).

The major source of the digital divide referred to in this paper is the the digital divide caused by visual impairment. A digital divide in the broader sense is the gap between those who have access to computers and the Internet and those who do not. Today's social activities and services have become increasingly digitized. Thus, there have been efforts from societies and governments to increase the social inclusion of disabled people in the realm of the Internet. However, much of the web over the Internet remains inaccessible for the visually impaired (Adam and Kreps 2006).

As mentioned earlier, there are four levels of visual function: normal vision, moderate visual impairment, severe visual impairment, and blindness (ICD 2006 as cited in WHO 2016a). Moderate visual impairment and severe visual impairment are categorized under "low vision". Visual impairment is the generic term given to all types of eye function problems of low vision and blindness. People under the low vision category use vision on a daily basis to perform a number of activities. Still, even after vision correction, low vision can interfere with an individual's capacity to undertake daily tasks (CEC 2000 as cited in Sapp 2003). Blindness is the term used to describe the condition of total sight loss in which the individual either does not see anything or can identify only darkness and light.

The specialized term legal blindness is associated with an acuity of 20/200 (i.e. the visually impaired person will see at 20 feet what a normal eyed person would see at 200 feet) and a visual field of less than 20 degrees. Although legal blindness describes a visual impairment, its use is mainly limited to individual eligibility for certain benefits (Koestler 1976, 45 as cited in Kelly et al. 2011).

The visual system is complex in nature, having different components working together to provide visual information to the brain. The major components include the sclera, cornea, iris, pupil, lens, retina, photoreceptor cells, optic disk, optic nerve, and visual cortex (Sapp 2003; Faye 1984 as cited in Kelly et al. 2011). Each of the above components has specialized functions, and significant damage to any of these components will cause visual impairment. Blindness is thought to exist due to reduced acuity, restricted visual fields, reduced contrast sensitivity, cortical damage, or other ocular dysfunction (Sapp 2003; Faye 1984 as cited in Kelly et al. 2011). According to WHO (2016a), the major global causes of visual impairment are uncorrected refractive errors such as myopia, hyperopia, or astigmatism (43%), unoperated cataracts (33%), and glaucoma (2%). Approximately 90% of people suffering from visual impairment live in developing countries and around 65% are aged 50 and above (WHO 2016a).

Visual impairment is the root cause for the digital divide, but today with the introduction of and advances in ICT, social inclusion is expected to rise. Denial of the truth obscures the root cause of the problem and this makes the problem persistent as it is empowered to overcome decisive attempts that were meant to resolve it, leaving VIP in darkness. Any social constructivist model that undermines the seriousness of visual impairment and thus the root cause of the digital divide, must be rejected. Instead, just as WHO (2016b) reported, working on social inclusion in terms of socio-economic development is recommended. This can be conceived by coordinating public health actions, making eye care services available, and increasing awareness among the general public about accessible medical treatments for treatable visual impairments. Moreover, a focus on inclusion in the fields of technological design, development, and production is also relevant.

The digital divide is a complex and multidimensional phenomenon that exists between and within countries (Bertot 2003 as cited in Sachdeva et al. 2015). The previous chapter discussed the major barriers involved in the creation of VID3, and there are a number of possible actions that could help to resolve it. First, increasing awareness among visually impaired patients, healthcare executives, healthcare providers, and manufacturers (i.e. the need for special and intelligent design, development, and production in order to minimize social exclusion by increasing inclusion in the production process). Second, to tackle the accessibility barrier with the adoption of new ICT technologies such as assistive technologies that are intended to increase social inclusion. Third, to diminish the motivational barrier by encouraging intended-purpose education to boost VIP motivation to use technology. Finally, to tackle healthcare information access barriers, which are illustrated in figure 1, after identifying and resolving technological, legislation, financial, and social factors which are the major benefactors to the creation of the barriers.

Healthcare information is important for visually impaired people to lead a healthy life. ICT devices, assistive software applications, and the Web together with the Internet are the major components of technology that need serious intervention to make them suitable for visually impaired people and to eradicate the VID3. The use of assistive technologies can play an important role in delivering alternative formats to the patient.

3.2 Assistive Technologies for the Visually Impaired

Those concerned should ask if the increased reliance on IT tends to continuously exclude people with disabilities whenever new developments occur. Thus, governments and blind institutes should work on the development and availability of assistive or adaptive applications and technologies. After the UN CRPD in 2007, there has been a rise in the development of affordable assistive technology in Europe. The UN CRPD aims at ensuring the rights and fundamental freedoms of disabled people by making assistive technologies affordable (Borg et al. 2011a; 2011b). Assistive technologies (ATs) include assistive, adaptive, and rehabilitative devices that are intended to support people with disabilities when performing activities. One of the most important practical applications of assistive technologies is in the arena of the Internet (Wills, Moumtzi, and Vontas 2010). Assistive technologies can reduce the barriers caused by disability when accessing the Internet and help improve lifestyle and achieve greater equality (Pal et al. 2011).

There are a number of useful assistive technologies for VIP, ranging from low-cost walking canes to expensive ICT devices. The visually impaired are a heterogeneous group, so depending on the severity of vision loss, the types of assistive technologies and output formats varies. The output format could be visual, auditory, or tactile. For example, text and image magnifiers are suitable for low-vision, tactile assistive technologies are recommended for blind and legally blind users, and tactile are used by deaf-blind users. The general purposes of these technologies include navigation and communication. Depending on the role of the assistive technologies, there are three major categories, namely back-end, input, and output.

Back-end tools perform operating system or application layer computing task such as translating scanned texts into machine language. Optical character recognition (OCR) does exactly this and is used together with other output technologies such as magnified text displayers and synthetic speech generators. The other set of useful back-end tools for VIP are braille translators, which are applications that bridge the operating system and braille output devices such as braille printers and displayers by creating braille readable files (NFB 2016). The description of OCR and braille translators, the major products available, and the cost range are provided in Table 1.

Table 1: Back-end assistive technologies for the visually impaired.

Back-end assistive technologies for Visually Impaired People (VIP)		
Assistive Device or Application	Products	Cost Range
Optical character recognition (OCR): This is the recognition of printed characters after converting it mechanically or electronically using photoelectric devices. There is open source and proprietary software.	Dynamsoft OCR SDK, Simple OCR, (a9t9), FreeOCR, Microsoft Document Imaging, One Note, CuneiForm, etc.	US$0–2000
Braille translators: These are programs containing algorithms that converts scripts into braille cells and send it to embossers. There are open source and proprietary translators available.	Index Direct Braille, Odt2Braille, Duxbury Systems' Braille, etc.	US$0–6000

Table 2: Input assistive technologies for the visually impaired.

Input Assistive Technologies for Visually Impaired People (VIP)		
Assistive Device or Application	Products	Cost Range
Speech Recognition (SR): This is composed of technologies that are capable of translating spoken language into text. This technologies are developed by the interdisciplinary field of computational linguistics.	LumenVox, Speech Engine, Braina, Tazti, Voice Finger 2.6.2, Dragon Naturally Speaking Professional, e-Speaking, Dragon for Mac, etc.	US$10–900
Braille Keyboards: This is an input device that enables users to type in texts to computers in the braille alphabet. It uses 8 keys, 6 for each braille dot, 1 for spaces and 1 more for special characters, etc. For VIP it is the equivalent of a standard keyboard.	MBraille, TypeinBraille, Braille Keyboard Cover, Braille Pen Slim, Portset Braillekey, Portset Braillekeyg2, Braille Pen 12, MaxiAids, Perkins Smart Brailler, Cosmo Braille Writer, etc.	US$0–2500

There must also be an interface between smart electronic devices, such as computers, and VIP in order to give instructions to the devices. Tools with this interfacing capability are categorized under input devices. Using these, people with various degrees of visual impairment interact with computing devices.

Table 3: Output assistive technologies for the visually impaired.

Output Assistive Technologies for Visually Impaired People (VIP)		
Assistive Device or Application	Products	Cost Range
Screen Readers: These are software applications interfacing operating systems, applications, and users that are capable of reading text documents displayed on the monitor of smart devices for VIP. There is open source and proprietary software.	System Access, Window-Eyes, JAWS (Job Access With Speech), and ZoomText Magnifier, NonVisual Desktop Access (NVDA), Serotek System Access, Applevoice Over (OS X), ORCA (Linux), BRLTTY (Linux), Emacspeak (Linux), WebAnyWhere (All OSs and Web Browsers), Spoken Web (Internet Explorer), ChromeVox (Google Chrome), ChromeVis (Google Chrome), etc.	US$0–1000
Speech Synthesizers: Systems designed to generate human speech that are found implemented in hardware and software products such as screen readers. There are free and paid ones.	DECtalk PC2, Eloquence, DoubleTalk, DECtalk Access32, Microsoft Speech Engine, eSpeak, etc.	US$0–1200
Braille embossers: Printers that use translation software to depict text as tactile braille, a hard copy in braille script of the original text.	Acoustic Hood Basic V4/V5, Acoustic Hood Everest V4/V5, Basic-D V5, Braille Embosser Basic-D V4, Braille Embosser Braille Boxpart, Braille, Embosser Everest-D V4, etc.	US$650–15000
Braille displays: Electro-mechanical device functioning as a terminal for displaying braille characters on a flat surface via raised pins as an output representing texts.	ALVA BC680, ALVA USB 640, Braille Star 40 and 80, Braille Wave, Brailliant B 80, Brailliant BI 40, Easy Braille, Focus 14 and 80 Blue Braille Display, Pac Mate, Seika, SuperVario, Sync Braille, Vario Ultra, Vario Connect, VarioPro, etc.	US$2000–12000
Screen magnifiers: Software that shows enlarged content.	MagnifyingGlass, DesktopZoom, OneLoupe, ZoomIt, Magnifixers, etc.	Free

Speech recognition (SR) and braille keyboards are among such devices. Speech recognition is used by both disabled and non-disabled people and is helpful for giving commands to devices (NFB 2016; Living Made Easy 2016). Braille keyboards are the equivalent of normal keyboards for visually impaired people. The details of speech recognition and braille keyboards, the major products available, and the cost range are provided in Table 2.

The final category is the output devices of visual, audio, and tactile ATs such as magnifiers, screen readers, and touch or haptic devices (Perkins School For Blind 2016; Index Braille 2016; UsabilityGeek 2016). These are devices that are used to send data from smart electronic devices to visually impaired people with any degree of severity of blindness including the deaf-blind people (NFB 2016). These technologies are very useful for this part of the community for communicating and performing their daily tasks. For example, for a deaf-blind person, the combination of the TTY (Text Telephone or TeleTypeWriter) and a braille display makes the use of the telephone possible, while simultaneously reading with the braille display. The TTY is appropriate for people with low-vision to communicate with others using larger fonts via large visual displays or computers (AADB 2009). The major output assistive technologies and products are described in Table 3.

3.3 Healthcare Information Sources and Accessible Formats

Healthcare information sources could play a significant role in helping VIP and other disabled people to maintain healthy and quality lives. This might bring about independent, confident, and zealous VIP, and groups of individuals capable of sparking innovative ideas for community facilities and services rather than merely accessing them. A study by Pal et al. (2011) concluded that there is a need for innovation and multi-disciplinary collaboration between researchers and experts working in the accessibility field. Additionally, the author of this paper believes that increasing the participation of VIP researchers would make innovation possible and, hence, add new values to the information accessibility industry. However, special attention must be given to innovations that can introduce new ways of designing and developing healthcare information sources capable of presenting healthcare information in an accessible format.

According to the United Nations (2007), the major barriers for people with disabilities include the scarcity of accessible information formats such as braille and sign language, stairs, and community services that are not understood by people with disabilities. The UN have urged for the application of accessible physical environments, transportation, information, and public facilities and services by all nations to maximize the quality of life for this group of individuals. These were the guiding principles for the implementation of the convention for accessibility by the UN for member states (UN 2007).

However, the emphasis of this thesis is VIP, and it will look further into the impact of advances in ICT on social inclusion and suggest how to diminish the VID3 effect. The major barriers—awareness, accessibility, and motivation—were explained in chapter two. The issue of inaccessible healthcare information formats is considered as the major type of the generic accessibility barrier that needs alternative formats to address the visually impaired. The existence of alternative or accessible formats would guarantee equal information access for all (Queen's University 2008). The following list shows vital healthcare information that needs to be delivered to visually impaired people in accessible formats according to NOLO (2016):

- Medical examinations and laboratory reports.
- Medical reports of disease diagnosis.
- Billing or payment methods.
- Privacy and security issues.
- Instructions for prescription medication that might contain important dosage information.
- Benefit eligibility information.
- Pregnancy and childbirth related information.
- Information on hospitals, referral doctors, and appointments.
- Other important healthcare-related information.

In some cases, there may already be accessible formats, but a lack of information about its existence, as mentioned earlier. After making alternative formats available, people need to be aware of it (Disabled Access Day 2016). For instance, a healthcare provider could hold standard material that explains to the visually impaired patient that there is an accessible format available and how to get it. Further, a proper request format must be prepared, and, once the patient issues the choice of format, there must already be a process in place that responds to the request (DHS 2016). An efficient healthcare information source can alleviate VID3 effects since it can provide the information to patients in their preferred format. The main accessible formats that are used to deliver healthcare information for VIP are presented in Table 4.

Table 4: Accessible information to everyone using accessible formats.

Accessible format type	Description	Output format
Large print	This is applicable for VIP and for people with learning disabilities. The font size should be at least 18pt. It is simply enlarged print.	Visual
Audio	Applicable for VIP and for people with learning disabilities. Audio can be delivered in a range of formats such as CD, cassette, and electronic or digital format (i.e. mp3, Daisy, DTB Opus, Vorbis, Musepack, AAC, ATRAC, and WMA). The audio need to include title, length, and content information, avoid noise in the speech, avoid background noise, record speech at a sensible speed, and describe images when they are involved.	Auditory
Braille	There are two types of Braille. The first, alphabetic braille, formerly called Grade One, writes out each letter and word exactly as it is spelled out in print. The second, literary braille, formerly called Grade Two, is also called contracted braille since it uses a single braille cell to print a word.	Tactile
Described video	It is a descriptive video read by a narrator in multimedia.	Auditory and visual
ePUB	It is a standard electronic book format. It enables eBooks in this format to be read on e-readers.	Auditory and visual
Electronic-text or E-text	These are the digital formats of Microsoft Word, Portable Document Format (PDF), PowerPoint, and Excel Spreadsheets.	Visual

3.4 Legislation and Policies on Disability Rights and Accessibility

3.4.1 The United States

As mentioned earlier, since 1966 Article 19 has made access to information a fundamental human right (ICCPR 1966 as cited in OHCHR 2016a). Additionally, Article 33 of the UN: The Convention on The Rights of Persons with Disabilities (CRPD) states that the disabled people have the right to information on an equal basis with others and through the form of communication of their choice (UN 2006). It has the potential to guide governments in discovering new ways to achieve social inclusion; in taking practical measures; and in drafting new policies and implementing them.

The convention will promote, protect, and ensure the rights of people with disabilities using its framework. When a country is to ratify and implement the convention, then it can be used in judicial and tribunal courts to fight any type of discrimination against the visually impaired. The UN General Assembly adopted the CRPD and the Optional Protocol in December 2006 and was internationally enforced in May 2008. Currently, there are 164 Parties to the Convention and 89 Parties to the Optional Protocol. The UN CRPD has been the most rapidly ratified treaty globally.

Human rights include rights and freedoms conceived and abstracted from issues such as dignity, fairness, equality, respect, and autonomy. This applies to information access; hence, every individual has the right to information that is timely, is in an accessible format, and has a high degree of relevance. The law must protect the right of people with disadvantages and prohibit discrimination against them. The European Union (EU) has a role in the implementation of the convention through its framework. The state parties must have a framework that promotes, protects and monitors the implementation of the UN CRPD. For this reason, the EU as a party to the convention has developed the framework for matters of the union's competence or for the actions taken by its member states to comply with the convention requirements. EU legislation and policy dealing with issues such as non-discrimination, and the EU's public administration dealing with issues such as accessibility, are among the issues supported by frameworks (European Commission 2015; FRA 2016).

The framework is currently composed of four major organizations: the European Parliament, the European Ombudsman, the EU Agency for Fundamental Rights (FRA), and the European Disability Forum (EDF). Its committee treaty body, is responsible for ensuring the rights of persons with disabilities. Its synergistic companion, the national monitoring framework, observes and adjusts implementation scenarios at the national level in the EU member countries. Normally, the companion is composed of other organizations, including the National Equality Bodies, which are under the European Network of Equality Bodies; the Ombudspersons, which are under the European Network of Ombudsmen; and the National Human Rights Institution, which is under the European Network of National Human Rights Institutions (European Commission 2015; FRA 2016). This paper will next cover the laws protecting the rights of people with disabilities and the fulfillment of the convention in the countries of interest.

The United States was the first country in the world to adopt national civil rights legislation and to ban discrimination against people with disabilities. Internationally, the UN CRPD consist of principles taken from The Americans with Disabilities Act (ADA) such as non-discrimination, equality of opportunity, accessibility, and inclusion. In the United States, all Federal agencies including the United States Department of Health and Human Services are required by law to make electronic information accessible to people with disabilities.

Section 508 (29 U.S.C. 794d) of the Rehabilitation Act of 1973 is the law that covers access to electronic information, and the amendment was passed by congress in 1998. Additionally, the American Foundation for the Blind (AFB) (2016) Section 508 was enacted to eliminate barriers within the information technology realm. This, in turn, will create opportunities for people with disabilities while leveraging resources needed for developing assistive technologies. The foundation understands that accessing information instantly without barriers of any kind will help individuals exercise their full abilities. Hence, the issue under Section 508 is making information accessible to disadvantaged people such as VIP with the same standard and quality as for the general public.

The ADA passed the law in 1990, which states that healthcare facilities must provide VIP healthcare information in alternative formats. The scope of this law is all healthcare providers, whether or not they are privately owned. This includes hospitals, private doctors' offices, health clinics, diagnostic centers, physical therapy centers, psychological and psychiatric service providers, and nursing homes. According to ADA (2016), the following are the requirements of the ADA law for healthcare facilities and providers:

- Healthcare facilities and providers must give VIP access to the same information that everyone else receives and should get care as effective as that provided to others.

- Alternative formats are legally required and auxiliary aids, services, and reading materials must be delivered using these formats by healthcare providers to patients, their companions, and VIP visitors.

- They must ensure effective communication between the provider, staff, and patients and must make available alternative formats without delay.

- The privacy of these patients and other patients with disabilities must be protected, and they should be allowed to act independently.

- Healthcare providers can make a decision regarding the type of information format the patient receives if it is a means of effective communication.

- Healthcare providers must consult with their patients to identify which format results in effective communication.

- Failing to provide alternative formats to these patients is a violation of federal laws by the healthcare provider.

- Healthcare providers must use available alternative formats or act independently and should not ask the patient to bring an interpreter or communication facilitator with them.

- Healthcare providers cannot rely on care-givers to facilitate communication.

3.4.2 Finland

The Ministry for Foreign Affairs of Finland (2016) has mentioned that the country agreed on May 11th, 2016 to pass into law the UN CRPD together with its optional protocol by June 10th, 2016. The ratification of the convention process was carried out with the Secretary-General of the United Nations and it is hoped it will promote the rights of people with disabilities. Most importantly, the core principle of the convention is the eradication of discrimination.

Moreover, it is hoped it will put to rest the discrimination VIP face and experience by serving as a counter civil rights legislation. What's more, it will help to officially recognize the convention and to increase its acceptance as legally binding human rights. Participants are also expected to continue promoting, protecting, and safeguarding the fundamental human rights and freedoms of people with disadvantages. The Ministry of Foreign Affairs led the group that prepared the ratification of the convention. According to the Ministry for Foreign Affairs of Finland (2016), other purposes of the ratification of the convention and the optional protocol together with the methodologies to be followed include:

- At the Committee's own initiative, procedures of individual communication and inquiry can be enabled via the Optional Protocol.

- To implement the convention, national level coordination will be first conceived by designing a center or focal points to deal with matters of this activity.

- For promoting, protecting, and monitoring the implementation, a national level framework will be developed.

Three different legislations, the Municipality of Residence Act, the Social Welfare Act, and the Act on Special Care for the Mentally Handicapped were affected by the ratification since it issued changes to be made. The Ministry of Social Affairs and Health (MSAH) deals with the issues of people with disabilities. Issues such as developing healthcare and social services and easing employment conditions are to be mentioned. The right to services is supported by the Social Welfare Act, the Disability Services Act, and the law on Intellectual Disabilities. Table 5 summarizes the organizations and their role in providing services for VIP in Finland.

Table 5: Finnish organizations and their role in providing services for VIP.

Name	Role
The Ministry of Social Affairs and Health (MSAH)	Responsible for promoting the welfare and health of people with disabilities and developing social and health services and income security.
Social Welfare Act, the Disability Services Act, and the law on Intellectual Disabilities	They require all disability rights including access to special services such as barrier-free housing, assistive devices, transport, and interpretation are met.
The National Institute for Health and Welfare (THL)	Promotes research and development on independent living for people with disabilities and barrier-free planning. Also, helps to collect disability related statistics, provides personal assistant, appropriate housing, and assistive devices.
The National Supervisory Authority on Welfare and Health (Valvira) and Regional State Administrative Agencies	Directing the execution of and provision of services and makes sure the standards for quality are met.
The National Council on Disability (VANE)	Promotes the rights of people with disabilities and cooperation between disability organizations and the authorities.

Generally, the matters of equality, participation, accessibility to necessary services, and support are taken into consideration in the Finnish policy for people with disabilities. Insufficient public services will be substituted with special services whenever possible to grant barrier-free environments for people with disadvantages. The municipality prepares almost all services needed for people with disabilities and even makes assistive technology available in healthcare centers. The services offered by the municipality include: transportation services; rehabilitation; support for informal care; service accommodation and institutional care; adaptation and rehabilitation guidance; financial support; disability benefits in association with the Social Insurance Institution of Finland, also called "Kansaneläkelaitos" or "Kela"; interpretation services; and employment (MSAH 2016).

3.4.3 Ireland

Ireland has yet to ratify and implement the United Nations Convention on the Rights of Persons with Disabilities, which the country signed in 2007 (Inclusion Ireland 2016). The report by the Irish Times on May 10, 2016, has stressed the seriousness of the task at hand and the unquestionable need for change (The Irish Times 2016b). The current law that governs decision making (i.e. Lunacy Regulations Act 1871) and the ward of the court system are the main barriers to ratification (Social Inclusion 2016). The Irish Times has reported on the extra weekly living costs (€207 to €276) for people with disadvantages (The Irish Times 2016a). This forces VIP and their families to live in poverty and excludes them from the community. Although the government has not yet ratified the UN CRPD (Longford Leader 2017), the intention is to include this task in the 2017 recovery budget in whichever way is possible, either by leveraging available resources or by optimizing existing resources.

Currently, there are laws protecting the basic rights of VIP and other people with disadvantages. Among these are the Employment Equality Acts 1998-2015; the Safety, Health, and Welfare at Work Act 2005; and the Disability Act 2005 (Citizens Information 2016). The Employment Equality Acts 1998–2015 prohibits discrimination in employment, training, and recruitment. It forces employers to fulfill the accommodation needs of employees with disabilities whenever necessary. However, this applies only if the costs of doing so are within the proportion set out under the EU legislation.

The Safety, Health, and Welfare at Work Act 2005 obligates employers to fulfill the needs of their employees with disabilities. The facilities of environments such as staircases, doors, passageways, showers and ICT systems such as workstations are referred to. Finally, the Disability Act 2005 requires all public bodies to attend to the needs of people with disadvantages by presenting electronic information in accessible format, for example. This is part of a framework of government legislative measures that are part of Ireland's National Disability Strategy supporting social inclusion (OHCHR 2016b).

3.4.4 The United Kingdom

The United Kingdom ratified the UN CRPD and the Optional Protocol in 2009. Since then the government has taken on initiatives to increase social inclusion. Nevertheless, in the UK, some fear that pushing the agenda so hard on the government might result in a reduction of the benefits that disabled people already enjoy. The country has set the UK Government's Office for Disability Issues (ODI) as its focal point to properly coordinate the implementation of the convention with human rights bodies. The UK Independent Mechanism (UKIM) for the convention has four independent designated bodies to monitor the implementation. These include the Equality and Human Rights Commission, the Scottish Human Rights Commission (SHRC), the Northern Ireland Human Rights Commission (NIHR), and the Equality Commission for Northern Ireland (ECNI).

The UK government together with the administrations of England, Scotland, Wales, and Northern Ireland observe the correct applications of all human rights within CRPD while implementing it. Promotion is mainly orchestrated via meetings and workshops via the ODI. Furthermore, The UK Disabled People's Council (UKDPC) uses a website to raise awareness about the convention and collect feedback on its implementation. The Human Rights Commission provides advice and information when enforcing the law and putting pressure on policies. Besides these, RNIB coordinates with VIP associations in the United Kingdom to measure the performance regarding the convention's implementation and report this to the UN Committee. The reports indicate that performance areas of the convention such as accessible information provision are weak and insufficient. More resources need to be leveraged in order to boost areas of accessible electronic information (EuroBlind 2016a).

The other, prominent act was The Disability Discrimination Act (DDA) of 1995. It was broad and did not address VIP health and social care information access problems in depth. The DDA act set high requirements and regulations on VIP to be covered. For these reasons, people with disabilities across the UK continued their campaign for change, resulting in the conception of the Disability Discrimination Regulations 2003 (SI No 712), which included Blind and Partially Sighted ones (US National Library of Medicine 2016). Until recently, this act served as the major ally for VIP by providing protection against discrimination on basic human rights issues such as accessible information provision.

3.4.5 France

France had other associations that help VIP in human rights issues long before the UN CRDP, which included the areas of information accessibility. Most of these institutes are categorized under the French Federation of the Blind and Visually Impaired (Fédération des Aveugles et Handicapés Visuels de France [FAF]), which was found in 1917 by Octave Berger (DBSV 2016).

France ratified the UN CRPD and the Optional Protocol in 2010. However, the country did not take actions to implement the convention immediately. In 2005 the act for equal rights, participation, citizenship, and opportunities received a great deal of attention; but, it was not until 2012 that the Prime Minister addressed the convention and 2013 that the General Secretary of the Inter-ministerial Committee on Disability dealt with it. The decision stated that the convention must be included in every parliamentary bill with the intention of changing public policies in favor of social inclusion. In addition to the ratification, special provisions must be given to VIP. The design of the focal points for all French ministries started on 2014 and is still involved in this process (EuroBlind 2016b). The coordination of the focal points and necessary measures to implement the UN CRPD are the roles of Inter-ministerial Committee. The roles of the French focal points for implementing the convention are as follows:

- Consulting government while drafting legislation, regulations, policies, and action plans.

- Evaluating the beneficial impact of the draft for the people with disabilities.

- Developing a disability diagnostic sheet and presenting it whenever new advances occur while implementing the convention.

- They will be mainly responsible for dealing with issues raised within society concerning disability.

The promotion of the UN CRPD in France is the duty of all major government institutes such as ministries, administrations, and local authorities. When it comes to monitoring the implementation of all international conventions such as the UN CRDP, a semi-external entity called the National Consultative Commission on Human Rights, the General Secretary of the Inter-ministerial Committee on Disability, the President of the National Advisory Council for Persons with Disabilities (Conseil National Consultatif des Personnes Handicapées), and the Defenders of Rights (Défenseur des Droits) are responsible.

The committee as a national authority plays a major role in ensuring the effective implementation of the rights in the UN CRPD and the provision of the convention in compliance with the laws. Practically, there are still barriers to the proper implementation of the convention. The courts in France did not yet let the scope of the convention prevail over the country's laws. Consequently, the French Council State have not yet decided to apply the convention (EuroBlind 2016b).

3.5 Information Systems and Strategies that Suit Visually Impaired People

3.5.1 Finland

This session deals with information system (IS) strategies that aimed to ease healthcare information access for VIP in a number of countries. These are ISs whose implementation has already added value or might add new value to this community. The previous session has shown that there are already legislation systems in place protecting the rights of people with disabilities. These are designed to protect, promote and monitor the rights of people with disabilities, including their healthcare information access rights (i.e. laws that prohibit discrimination on the basis of disability and disparities in the system).

The laws also demand healthcare information to be delivered to this group of individuals in an information format that they can understand. This is why the right to request healthcare information in alternative formats is also perceived as a fundamental human right and is supported by governments both locally and globally. In the healthcare realm, proper communication between visually impaired patients and providers is, therefore, decisive in bringing about a high-quality healthcare system. To improve the healthcare communication between providers and the visually impaired, there are useful strategies worth sharing. Although these strategies do not specifically target the healthcare industry, the scope of their applicability is very large and will extend to this industry as well.

In Finland, the Finnish Federation of the Visually Impaired (FFVI) or näkövammaisten liitto ry (NKL) gives support and encourages VIP to participate in the information society (FFVI 2016). The purpose of these efforts is to eradicate the barriers to information access and ease the daily activities of reading, writing, and communication via smooth interactions with ICTs. The association plans to establish the effective management of the information society.

In the scientific arena, the National Institute of Health and Welfare (THL) takes on the research and development in order to encourage independent living by the visually impaired while simultaneously helping to remove barriers. To do so, it also runs the Finnish Register of Visual Impairment program together with näkömmaisten liitto ry and keeps statistics of VIP in Finland (Ojamo and Uusitalo 2012). In 2011, the population in Finland was 5.4 million, of which the number of the visually impaired was 80,000 (FFVI 2016). Chart 1 illustrates the causes of visual impairment and their share, in percent, of the total 80,000.

Chart 1: The Finnish register of visual impairment for the year 2011.

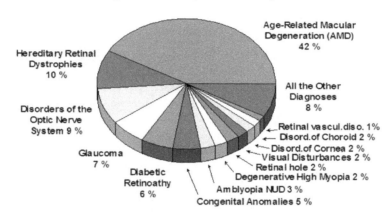

Source: The Finnish Register of Visual Impairment, 2012.

The aims of the annual program are mainly to prevent and treat visual impairment, provide rehabilitation programs, and other special services for VIP. In the IS realm, Näkömmaisten liitto ry's intended purpose is to promote the social inclusion of VIP and deaf-blind people through the information society. Hence, ICT facilities, including healthcare and different information sources, are to be accessible and available. This, in turn, makes alternative formats accessible whilst giving the capability for these people to communicate and produce information independently. In order to accomplish this, the association has come up with a four years strategic plan, that covered 2012 to 2016 (FFVI 2012).

If successful, by the end of 2016, the main communication channel for VIP will be an electronic and digital information network system. Also the Digital Accessible Information System (DAISY) and large print are to be synchronized with emails. Emphasis will be given to the impact of mobile devices on the management of information, different transactions, and social interactions. These information management network systems are to use assistive technologies to ease access to the visually impaired and affordable broadband connections for data processing. The assistive technologies will be either visual or auditory depending on the choice of the visually impaired person. Moreover, these technologies will be made available in all locations to all groups of the visually impaired on an equal basis. These efforts will result in a higher number of the visually impaired using computers with assistive technologies such as speech synthesizers, easy-to-use terminals, and mobile hardware technologies. These are able to provide electronic services that in turn enable the visually impaired to take advantage of social media.

Additionally, to cope with the increased complexity in information systems there will be a need for barrier-free working environments and the knowledge to achieve this. Easily accessible training centers will be available, near to the user's place of residence, and the most suitable training will be delivered after their information input-output format preference is known. Training and access to assistive devices will be available in work places. In these places, the rights of VIP work role will be respected and strengthened with the help of appropriate education for all staff. Braille has also become an increasingly necessary tool for communicating while working and studying in digital and paper formats. Its application extends to the management of the home environment, product packaging, signs, elevators, means of transport, and public buildings.

This association is part of the Finnish DAISY consortium, working together to ease the daily life of the visually impaired. The consortium includes Celia; Näkövammaisten kirjastoyhdistys ry or the Library Association of the Visually Impaired; Keskuspuiston ammattiopisto or Keskuspuisto Vocational College; Förbundet Finlands Svenska Synskadade r.f. or the Federation of Swedish Speaking Visually Impaired in Finland (FSVIF); and Kolibre r.f. (DAISY Suomen DAISY konsortio 2016). Kolibre r.f., for example, aims at producing custom information systems that are suitable for people with disabilities, including VIP. To do this, the organization itself has engaged in research and development in the IS field and supports other IS projects with a similar goal (Kolibre 2016). Others, such as FIMEA, in marketing authorizations advocate the use of braille for proper labeling and packing while using leaflets for medicinal products (FIMEA 2015).

3.5.2 The United Kingdom

The UK have made direct and explicit efforts to make healthcare information accessible for VIP. The Royal National Institute of Blind (RNIB) is the predominant organization that has helped the visually impaired since 1868 with its first goal of enhancing embossed literature. The organization has been known by different names and only became the RNIB in 2002. Since then, the organization has helped VIP in different aspects of life. By 1935, it already provided talking book services for children. Later, large print news and television listings called the "big print newspaper" were developed (RNIB 2016).

In 2014, in a population of 64.1 million there were almost 2 million VIP in the UK. The major causes of visual impairment are age macular degeneration (AMD), cataract, diabetic retinopathy (DR), and glaucoma. The number of the visually impaired is increasing in the country; by 2020 it will reach 2.25 million and by 2050 will be about 4 million (UK Vision Strategy 2014). Chart 2 below illustrates the projected number of VIP in the United Kingdom:

Chart 2: Projected number of VIP (in millions) in the UK.

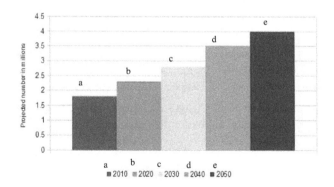

Source: The chart is based on the data obtained from Access Economics 2009 as cited in UK Vision Strategy 2014.

The RNIB understands the need for increased social inclusion as the number of VIP increases significantly. The organization is working on various areas of life to help and support people with disadvantages. In the areas of health and social care services, it is currently working on the accessibility of information for visually impaired customers. In September 2014, the organization held a seminar with the National Health Service

(NHS) England with the aim of making health and social care information accessible to these group of people. A persuasion campaign was designed with the intention of making information accessible and its hearing process lasted until mid-November of the same year. In the seminar held during the campaign, they conceived what is called the "Accessible Information Standard" (RNIB 2014b).

The aim was to use this Accessible Information Standard to pressure health and social care service providers in a number of ways. First, to find their visually impaired customer's preferred means of communication. Second, to identify and use suitable alternative formats. Finally, to record VIP's preferred means of communication. The scope of the campaign was limited to health and social care information. It did not intend to remove the barriers within display signs, website accessibility, and health and social care workers' attitudes (RNIB 2014b).

In June 2016, after almost two years, all NHS service providers were obliged by law to follow the Accessible Information Standard. The ultimate purpose of the standard is to establish effective communication between VIP and their health and social care workers. It is composed of accessible information specifications and implementation guidance. For effective implementation of the standard, the following strategies were devised:

- Policies will be reformed with the concept of disability equality.

- Standard procedure must be conceived to implement the policies.

- Re-education will be needed to bring about attitudinal change among health and social care workers.

- Existing electronic systems will need to be customized so as to suit people with disadvantages.

If successful, the RNIB and NHS will manage to establish the effective communication system they are aiming for. In other words, the NHS will possess custom ICT facilities that enable health and social care services to address VIP healthcare information needs. In the revived system, a two-way communication system will be made available for patients to contact and to be contacted by providers via services such as email, text relay, and text message. Patients will receive information they understand, using alternative formats such as audio, braille, and large print. The report on the implementation of the Accessible Information Standard will be published around March 2017 (NHS 2016; RNIB 2014b).

3.5.3 France

In France, the main organization dealing with the needs of VIP is the French Federation of the Blind and Visually Impaired (FAF). Founded in 1917, the federation aims at improving the moral, intellectual, and social status of the visually impaired in France and abroad by defending their rights. There are 44 associations under it, while the federation is itself a member of the French National Committee for the Welfare of the Blind and Visually Impaired, the European Blind Union, the Francophone Union of the Blind, and the World Blind Union. Among FAF activities and contributions are the support of VIP in areas of life, pursuing innovative approaches, and employment issues and has assisted 100 VIP annually to get guide dogs. Furthermore, it is the co-founder of BrailleNet and the Helen Server, a virtual library for VIP, and with its Access Formation program it is training the visually impaired to live independently (DBSV 2016).

Most of the legal concerns regarding information accessibility, such as social and healthcare, are the responsibilities of French Confederation for the Social Promotion of Blind and Partially Sighted (Confédération Française pour la Promotion Sociale des Aveugles et Amblyopes [CFPSAA]) (EuroBlind 2016b). In 2013, of the 66 million French population, about 1.7 million were VIP. The major causes of visual impairment included glaucoma, cataracts, diabetic retinopathy, age-related macular degeneration, and a refractive problem such as myopia, hypermetropia, astigmatism, and presbyopia. Healthcare professionals in the country have started to work on enhancing community care with the emergence of multidisciplinary networks situated in the same area (OPC 2016).

There are efforts from Public Health France—specifically the National Institute of Prevention and Education for Health (INPE) and National Solidarity Fund for Autonomy (CNSA)—to make healthcare information accessible to VIP in France. Together they have published two guidelines, namely Inform the Deaf and Inform the Visually Impaired (INPES 2013). The institute has been active since 2008 in the area of information accessibility for the visually impaired and other people with disabilities. As a result, the organization was able to come up with guidelines that are accessible online, on the website of INPE, either in HTML or PDF formats. In addition to these, the institute understands the need for universal accessibility. For this reason, the institute is planning to run a site on universal access in order to inform about a tool-set that is understandable by all. The INPE have emphasized the lack of global initiatives in the area of the healthcare information needs of VIP and other people with disabilities (INPES 2013).

3.5.4 Ireland

Since 1931, the National Council for the Blind of Ireland (NCBI) has been supporting and providing services for VIP in the Republic of Ireland. In 2012, the country's population was around 4.58 million and there were around 15,000 VIP. Of those VIP using the services of this organization, 5% were completely blind and 95% had varying degree of impairment (Informing Families 2016). Among those organizations actively making services accessible to people with disabilities, O'Herlihy Access Consultancy (OHAC) should be mentioned. It consults with both local and international clients to make all of their services accessible for all (OHAC 2016).

The National Disability Authority (NDA) participates in policy making, developing standards and codes of practices, and in their implementation. For example, it gives support to the Minister for Justice and Equality while at the same time drafting disability policy. It is also known to promote Design for All principles such as universal design to make environments, services, and ICT facilities easily accessible to all (NDA 2016).

The Health Service Executive (HSE) is an organization that is also involved in the delivery of social and healthcare services. The HSE actively participates in the conception and promotion of the National Guidelines on Accessible Health and Social Care Services (HSE 2016). The organization is directly involved in making healthcare information accessible for VIP. It recommends that healthcare providers establish the visually impaired patient's preferred method of communication, notify staff about it, and provide the accessible format for the patient that they can review at home if needed (HSE 2016).

3.5.5 The United States of America

There are a number of organizations that have been helping VIP in the United States such as the American Foundation for Blind (AFB), which was established in 1921. This organization's main goal is to ensure access to ICT, educational, and legal services for the visually impaired, and to help them to lead an independent life. Currently, the major activities of the AFB for VIP can be summarized as finding innovative ways to make information accessible with the help of assistive technologies; advocating their rights; and ensuring equal opportunities in different areas of life (AFB 2016). Another organization is the American Council of the Blind (ACB), which has had affiliates under different names since 1880. This organization's main goal is to increase VIP's quality of life by providing equal opportunities, while enabling VIP to live independently (ACB 2016).

In 2014, the United States had a population of 318.9 million, an estimated of 20 to 25 million of whom were VIP (CDC 2009; AFB 2015). The major causes of visual impairment are: cataract, diabetic retinopathy (DR), glaucoma, and advanced age-related macular degeneration (AMD). Within the next 30 years or so, the number of VIP in the United States is expected to double. Recent research by the Centers for Disease Control and Prevention (CDC) indicate that diabetes related visual impairment is likely to escalate rapidly in the coming four decades (CDC 2009). Chart 2 below demonstrates the projected number of VIP while considering the causes for visual impairment. This estimate is from the CDC's 2009 statistics. The data shows that the total number of VIP in the year 2020 will grow to 43.5 million. However, this number might vary greatly due to the migration of people into the country.

Chart 3: Projected number of VIP (in millions) in the USA by cause of impairment.

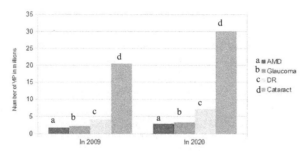

Source: Data to draw the chart obtained from CDC VIP statistics 2009.

There are already federal laws in the United States requiring healthcare information to be provided in an accessible format or in a format a visually impaired person understands. There have also been government initiatives to make healthcare information accessible to the visually impaired in the country. Despite these efforts, the non-compliance problem remains unsolved. Meanwhile, inaccessible prescription information is affecting the health of the visually impaired for a number of reasons. These include the difficulties the visually impaired faces when trying to distinguish between various medicine packages and finding the expiration date and the dosage. The report by the Equal Rights Center of (2011) as cited in NOLO (2016) reveals that only 1% of pharmacies and retailers are complying with the law; the rest do not provide prescription information in auxiliary formats. This and other forms of discrimination against VIP in terms of making healthcare information accessible remains unsolved (NOLO 2016).

4 RESEARCH PROCESS

4.1 Research Methodology

The topic and the research questions together influenced the author to use a mixed research method approach. In this research, both qualitative and quantitative research methods were used. Qualitative research was crucial due to the need for an in-depth study of the topic that obtains the best interpretations and understandings of the underlying problems. A general method similar to discourse analysis was used to understand visual impairment itself and its impact on information accessibility. Also, with increased digitization and advances in ICT, the arena of HCIA for VIP is undoubtedly influenced by social constructs that can be explained in the context of IS. For this reason, the qualitative philosophical stance of critical research was adopted. Together, this necessitated an intensive literature review.

With the limited resources at hand, What other, way to qualify the research, other than using the literature, especially, that which has the potential to be used as secondary data sources. Early in the project, a literature review of selected articles and journals was conducted and a profound knowledge and understanding of the research topic was developed. During the literature review, potential areas of research and relevant earlier studies on the topic were identified. This, in turn, helped to identify the knowledge gaps and the corresponding investigations required to address them. Meanwhile, the findings of previous studies were carefully documented. This made the contrast between previous research and the findings of this paper clear.

To ensure that the barriers and the factors associated with VIP HCIA problems, and the associated digital divide, were identified, it was vital to use quantitative research methods. However, this were not the only reason for using this research method. It was understood that the barriers identified with a quantitative method—namely awareness, accessibility, and motivational barriers—and the factors causing them to exist social, technological, financial or economic, and legal are common in today's cyber-enabled world. As a result, these findings can be generalized to the larger global VIP population.

4.2 Data Collection

4.2.1 Survey of visually impaired people's institutes in Europe

In this project, a combination of primary and secondary data sources is used. For the qualitative aspect of the study, secondary data sources such as documents from the literature and online or digital materials were utilized. This data helped to perform an explanatory research and to further develop the thoughts that became the basis for the quantitative section of the research. This method enabled the author to explore the different aspects of the HCIA problems. For example, the major barriers for HCIA and the associated factors were identified. These barriers can be eliminated while reshuffling the factors involved in favor of VIP. Visual impairment itself has been the major source of the digital divide. However, with the staggering advances in ICT, the digital divide can be bridged and increased social inclusion can be realized. This is true for all aspects of life, including the delivery of accessible HCI for the visually impaired. Furthermore, the advances in ICT will have a positive impact on the efforts being made to meet the healthcare information needs of the visually impaired. However, this is not true; even when looking at most of the EU countries that are equipped with advanced technologies.

This led to the hypothesis that, despite the staggering advances in ICTs in today's world, even in the most developed parts of the world such as Europe, the healthcare information needs of VIP are not being met, even in the most developed parts of the world such as Europe. This hypothesis is made on the basis of limited evidence and will serve as a starting point for further investigation. The details of the hypothesis testing and the findings are found in the results and discussion sections.

The quantitative part of the research was exploratory in nature. It tends to seek explanations and provide evidence for the hypothesis. A survey was chosen as the means to collect data and to test the hypothesis. Additionally, credible online resources were used to collect secondary data. Before conducting the survey, it was mandatory to identify the population of interest. After careful consideration and discussion with the supervisor, the population of interest was chosen.

The non-random sampling method was used to choose the participants. This made the recruitment process easier and precise. Using the recruitment process, the best possible delegates for the visually impaired were chosen as participants. After this, a questionnaire with 10 questions was prepared and sent out to the participants. The aim was to make a sound conjecture about the healthcare information needs of the wider visually impaired population in Europe based on the data collected. Details of the survey life cycle are found in the next section.

The population of interest was the national organizations, federations, or institutes of blind and partially sighted people in European countries. Most of the contacts were found from the European Blind Union (EBU). The EBU have 44 member countries, each of which is represented by a national delegation. This was followed by the collection of data from the target using a standardized form of the questionnaire.

The questionnaire (see Appendix 1) was ready for production on February 2nd, 2016, using online survey software called Webpropol. The first batch of the survey was sent out to 49 contacts selected from 29 EBU member countries via email. The email was sent out on February 23, 2016 and contained a cover letter and a link to the online survey page of the webpropol (see Appendix 2). About 22 days were given for the recipient to fill out the questionnaire. During this period of time, there were no responses to the questionnaire. Although the research team did anticipate the probability of getting responses to be small, the overall number of response did surprise the team. Of course, the team was aware of securing a high response rate to this kind of survey will be relatively difficult. While selecting the participants the method of the recruitment used was the electronic mail. Factors such as length and content of questionnaire and the level of intimacy between respondents and researchers play an important role in getting high response rate. For these reasons, all possible precautionary measures were taken, including:

- The research questions were to the point, as they were mindfully planned.
- The layout of the questionnaire was carefully designed and the questionnaires were clear and well presented.
- Both open and closed questions were used whenever appropriate in the research tool.
- Semi-piloting tests had been carried out before sending out the survey.
- The email sent out to the recipients had a cover letter explaining the purpose of the survey and other important remarks.
- Non-random sampling was used to make the data collection processes easier, the population of interest was chosen, and the participants were recruited by mail.
- The target sample size was made relatively small and this was done after taking the goal of the study and the resources available into account.

Nevertheless, the response rate was poor and this was really surprising for the research team. Because, all of the participants are national delegates of the European Blind Union and just imagine their slogan says, "The voice of blind and partially sighted people in Europe". Given these federations, institutes, and organizations are put in place mainly for the purpose of uplifting VIP in different aspects of life and to help them in experiencing the same quality of life as their fellow citizens, the level of participation the delegates showed was relatively poor.

The second batch of the survey was sent out on March 15, 2016, to the same recipients. This time the research team gave a five day interval to fill out the questionnaire, making March 20th, 2016 the deadline. During this period, only one respondent from Finland responded to the survey. The recipient from the FFVI or NKL responded on March 16, 2016. Table 6 shows the information obtained from the VIP delegate of Finland. The response regarding the questionnaire that asks about the existence of special legislation, policies, processes, or systems put in as Incentives for HCIA in Finland include:

- The European Accessibility Act and the Operational Programme, which ran from 2011 to 2015 with the slogan, "towards an accessible information society".
- The Ministry of Transport and Communications with JHS 129 principles of public administration for web services quality criteria within network design and implementation.
- The accessibility indicators as an instrument for development and evaluation of online public services from the Ministry of Finance and Communications and the Ministry of Transport and Communications.
- The Disability Policy Programme that ran from 2012 to 2015.
- The Finnish Design for All program by Network Radius (electronic service and democracy enhancement).
- The nationwide obligations to mark medicine packages with braille text.

A third and final attempt to collect data was made on March 31, 2016. This was again to the same recipients. The third batch of the survey had an eight day interval, with a deadline of April 8th, 2016. Once again, during this period, there was only one respondent: the recipient from Ireland, on April 1st, 2016, used email to fill out the questionnaire. Table 7 shows the information obtained from the VIP delegate of Ireland.

The response rate of the survey was 4.08%, and was calculated as follows:

$r=(n'/n)*100, r=(2/49)*100$

Here, r, n', and n are the number of response rate, number of responses, and number of total sent out, respectively. In this particular case, the numerical value for n is 2 and for n' is 49.

Table 6: The survey on the healthcare information needs of the Finnish visually impaired.

Incentives for healthcare information accessibility	Finland
Internet resources that deliver HCI with special arrangements for VIP of a specific country.	Terveyskirjasto (URL: terveyskirjasto.fi) and Omahoitopolut (URL: omahoitopolut.fi).
Companies/Organizations that deliver HCI with special arrangements for VIP.	The Finnish Medical Society Duodecim (URL:duodecim.fi/english); National Institute for Health and Welfare (URL: thl.fi/en/web/thlfi-en); The Finnish pharmacy system (URL: apteekki.fi); and From public health at least two, namely The Finnish Diabetes and Heart Disease.
Assistive technologies put in place to help VIP access HCI.	Screen reading program, Speech software, and braille display.
If policies, processes, and systems designed take into account the different demographic conditions of VIP.	The severity of blindness of blind and partially sighted persons has been somewhat taken into consideration. No information on the rest such as gender, age, level of education, socio-economic groups, and geographic location.
Economic and other support measures taken to support internet access of VIP.	Computer aids are free of charge for visually impaired persons.
Measures supporting VIP in their access to HCI.	At the Finnish Federation for Visually Impaired (FFVI), the use of Internet in general is supported and taught in courses. Also during vision rehabilitation, computer and internet skills are taught. The federation also works with different organizations on issues concerning accessibility, provides information on accessibility, and does advocacy work.
NB: Web accessibility for VIP is unknown as there are no data sets, but the obligation to mark medicine packages with braille text has been considered as special legislation.	

Table 7: The survey on the healthcare information needs of the Irish Visually Impaired.

Incentives for healthcare information accessibility	Ireland
Internet resources that deliver HCI with special arrangements for VIP of a specific country.	No data obtained.
Companies/organizations that deliver HCI with special arrangements for VIP.	At least one, the NCBI.
Assistive technologies put in place to help VIP access HCI.	Braille, audio, and large print.
Special legislation, policies, processes, or systems put in place to satisfy the HCI needs of VIP.	The Disability Act 2005, public bodies are obliged to give information in accessible formats, obligatory to mark medicine packages with braille text, and public bodies must ensure that their online services are accessible.
Education to help VIP to get access to HCI.	NCBI Braille certificate course is given as a qualification expected from public service providers.
If policies, processes, and systems designed take into account the different demographic conditions.	No information.
Obligation to mark medicine packages with braille text.	Yes, it is obligatory.
Economic and other support measures taken to support internet access of VIP.	No information.
Measures supporting VIP in their access to HCI.	NCBI Media Centre converts information and documents into formats accessible for a range of voluntary, public, and private organizations including audio, braille, clear print, and Braille certificate course.

NB:There are no details on web accessibility. Only the number of services and web sites were obtained from the respondent during the survey.

4.2.2 Secondary data on ICTs

Table 8 is from a secondary data source: values were obtained from the Global Information Technology Report of the World Economic Forum of 2014. In the table, the code "1" depicts the ordinal scale "not at all" and the code "7" depicts the ordinal scale "to a great extent". The weighted average data is from the year 2012 to 2013 (World Economic Forum 2014).

Table 8: Taken from the global networked readiness index 2014, showing ICT performance of Finland and Ireland.

ICT performance indicator	Acronym for the performance indicator	Finland	Rank out of 148	Ireland	Rank out of 148
Accessibility of digital content	ADC	5.4	14	4.6	46
Availability of latest technologies	ALT	6.5	2	5.4	49
Impact of ICT on access to basic services	IAS	6.5	1	5.9	30
Laws relating to ICTs	LICT	5.7	10	4.7	44
Government procurement of advanced technologies	GPAT	5.6	5	5.1	23
Quality of educational system	QES	4.2	21	3.5	70
Capacity for innovation	CI	5.9	2	5.5	5
Affordability	AF	5.7	2	4.6	20
Skills	SLS	6.4	18	4.7	98
Extent of staff training	EST	6.5	1	6.1	9
Government success in ICT promotion	GS	5.5	2	4.8	20
ICT use and government efficiency	ICTG	5.3	16	4.7	41

4.3 Data Analysis

4.3.1 Descriptive analysis

The information obtained from the Finnish and Irish respondents was studied. First, the questions within the survey questionnaire sorted into its type of IHCIA. Second, for each IHCIA identified, the appropriate acronym was formulated (see Appendix 3). Finally, this was followed by the tabulation of the raw data, which resulted in a "1" or "0" coding and quantity based categories. In the first category, every IHCIA response with one or more instances were coded as "1", meaning that a particular IHCIA exists. Those with a zero number of instances in the response were coded as "0", meaning the absence of that particular IHCIA. In the second category, the number of IHCIA instances for each IHCIA type in each response was counted. Table 9 shows the responses of the Finnish and the Irish delegates after the tabulation process.

Table 9: The responses to the survey on the HCI needs of VIP in categories for both countries.

IHCIA Type	Finnish 1st category	Finnish 2nd category	Irish 1st category	Irish 2nd category
	Code ['1'=exist |'0'=does not exist]	The number of IHCIA instances in the response counted	Code ['1' =exist |'0'=does not exist]	The number of IHCIA instances in the response counted
IR	1	Two	0	Zero
OS	1	Five	1	One
AT	1	Three	1	Three
LPS plus BMO	1	Seven	1	Four
ESA	0	Zero	1	One
DCD	1	One	0	Zero
EIA	1	One	0	Zero
MSA	1	Seven	1	Two
BMO	1	One	1	One

Given the small data sample available, the author had to decide on the most suitable techniques for further analysis. The analysis should first go through techniques that are descriptive by nature. The data was analyzed in terms of the number of IHCIA instances that used the data in category 2 (seen in Table 9) to obtain the relationship shown in Chart 4. The chart suggests that Finland might be performing well in regard to fulfilling the HCI needs of its VIP citizens. Nevertheless, for a number of reasons listed below, this conclusion is uncertain.

- The lack of the sampling distribution of a large data sample prevents the evaluation of the mean value for each type of IHCIA category.
- The responses from the Finnish delegate did not assure web accessibility for VIP, implying that the number of IHCIA instances could vary.
- Neither respondent filled out the questionnaire completely, if so, the result could have been different.

Thus, although the results developed from the descriptive data analysis of category two does give a glimpse of the reality, it lacks the required level of credibility and further analysis is needed.

Chart 4: Comparison between Finland and Ireland in terms of the number of IHCIA instances.

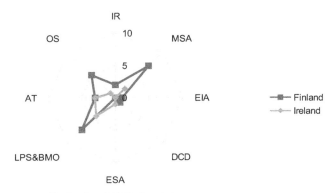

Another way to analyze the data is to study the relationship between the two countries' data in terms of the existence and absence of IHCIA. To achieve this, Chart 5 was produced using the data from category one. However, this is only descriptive and needs further analysis for the same reasons listed earlier.

Chart 5: Comparison between Finland and Ireland in terms of the existence of IHCIA.

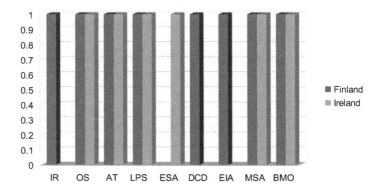

Table 10: The 2012–2013 ICT performance indicators of Finland and Ireland.

ICT performance indicator	Finland	Ireland
ADC	5.4	4.6
ALT	6.5	5.4
IAS	6.5	5.9
LICT	5.7	4.7
GPAT	5.6	5.1
QES	4.2	3.5
CI	5.9	5.5
AF	5.7	4.6
SLS	6.4	4.7
EST	6.5	6.1
GS	5.5	4.8

According to data obtained from the 2014 World Economic Forum, Finland has better key performance indicators in terms of the availability, affordability, accessibility, usability, etc. of ICTs. This secondary source is credible enough to be used for data analysis purposes. The information displayed in Table 8 was simplified to acquire only the performance indicator values. As shown in Table 10 above, only acronyms are used to depict each indicator (see Appendix 4). Chart 6 below, which is based on the data in Table 10, graphically illustrates ICT performance indicator values for the two countries.

Chart 6: The comparison between the two countries in terms of performance indicator values of ICT.

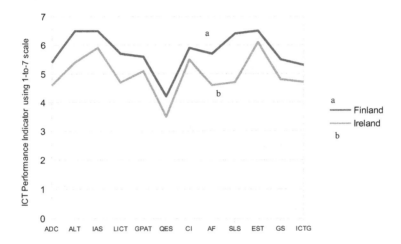

The performance indicators that can best explain the variation in the number of instances of a particular type of IHCIA was examined. To do this, first, the relationship between these two must be studied to determine whether or not they possess a one-to-many relationship. The findings from this will be used as a basis for providing a pragmatic solution in the accessible healthcare information realm. For example, the availability of Internet resources that deliver healthcare information with special arrangements for VIP of a specific country, can be affected by ICT performance indicator values of "accessibility of digital content" and "the impact of ICT on access to basic services and capacity for innovation", as shown in Figure 2 below.

Figure 2: The one-to-many relationship between IHCIA and ICT performance indicators.

Source: The author's work, based on the 2012–2013 ICT Performance Indicators report by the World Economic Forum 2014.

However, this is only theoretical and in order to arrive at precise results, a further study must be made. The study might need to, first, categorize these ICT performance indicators into the respective factors that contribute to HCIA barriers in the context of IS, namely social, technological, financial or economic, and legal. This should be followed by the acquisition of large data sets to perform multivariate regression statistical analysis. This is because the relationship between the number of IHCIA instances and ICT performance indicators is one-to-many. However, with the current data available for this research, it is more meaningful to analyze the data using simple regression analysis, which is covered in the next section.

4.3.2 Inferential analysis

The author did not yet possess or produce strong evidence to make claims such as:

- Finland has a better healthcare information system (HCIS) with higher social inclusion values than Ireland.

- The reason behind Finland's better performance in fulfilling the healthcare information needs of the visually impaired is directly related to the country's overall excellent ICT performance.

- Finland is showing strong efforts to fulfill the HCI needs of VIP in proportion to its great advances in ICT and digital data management.

- Advances in ICT and the increased technological capacity of the developed areas of Europe is helping to leverage resources for the HCI needs of VIP.

For these reasons, the data was approached through an analysis that is inferential by nature has become mandatory. At the end of the previous section, a one-to-many relationship among the number of IHCIA instances and ICT performance indicators was identified. However, it was also explained that there is a lack of sampling distribution; with the current data available for this research it was reasoned that the data should be analyzed using simple regression analysis. In this particular case, the dependent and the independent variables are the number of IHCIA instances and the ICT performance values, respectively. Thus, a simple regression analysis technique will be used to study the assumed one-to-one relationship that exists between ICT performance indicator values and the number of IHCIA instances. Here, the indicator was hypothetically matched with its corresponding incentive. This was done by taking into account the degree to which a particular indicator value could best explain the variation in the number of instances of the corresponding specific HCIA type. This resulted in one-to-one relationship data, which is shown in Table 11.

Table 11: Round-up mean values for IHCIA and ICT performance values of Finland and Ireland.

IHCIA instances	1	3	3	5	1	1	3	5
ICT performance indicator	5	5.4	5.6	5.2	5.6	5	5.2	6.3

Chart 7 below illustrates the relationship between the two variables while using the mean values shown in Table 11. The value of the correlation coefficient R is the radical of the coefficient of determination or R^2 and can be used to ascertain the strength of the relationship between the two variables. The round-up value of R after computing is 0.52, suggesting a relatively weak relationship for the scientific standard, which is 0.8. The coefficient of determination is 0.3, suggesting that only 30% of the total variation in the number of IHCIA instances can be explained by the linear relationship between the number of instances and the performance indicators. Similar regression analysis was performed on the data from Finland and Ireland separately.

Chart 7: The overall relationship between IHCIA and ICT performance of both countries.

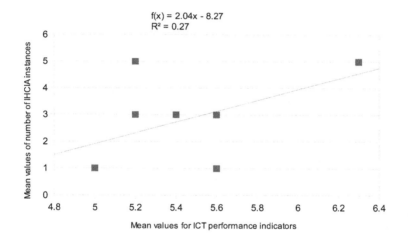

Tables 12 below contains the values depicting the assumed one-to-one relationship of an IHCIA and its corresponding indicator for Finland. It is vital to visualize the effect of the difference in indicator values on the number of incentives for HCIA instances of the two countries separately. There is an explanation of the validity of these data earlier, in section 4.3.1.

Table 12: The Finnish variation in the number of IHICA as the indicator values change.

IHCIA instances	2	5	3	6	1	1	0	7
ICT performance indicator	5.4	5.6	6.5	5.7	6.4	5.3	5.7	6.5

According to Chart 8 below, the relationship between the two variables has become even weaker. It is only safe to propose that the relationship between the two variables is non-random and non-linear. The round-up value of the correlation coefficient is 0.28, signifying a weak relationship between the two variables. The value of the coefficient of determination is 0.08, implying that the linear relationship can only explain 8% of the total variation in the number of HCIA instances.

Chart 8: The Finnish relationship between the number of IHCIA instances and ICT performance indicators.

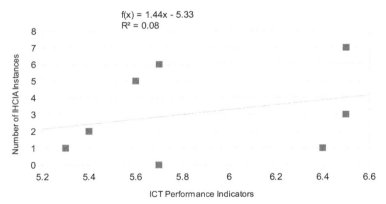

Table 13 demonstrates that a one-to-one relationship exists between IHCIA and its corresponding indicator in terms of the numerical values for Ireland. Reflections were made earlier in this section about the validity of each datum.

Table 13: The Irish variation in the number of IHICA instances as the indicator values change.

IHCIA instances	0	1	3	3	0	0	1	2
ICT performance indicator	4.6	5.1	5.4	4.7	4.7	4.7	4.6	6.1

In Chart 9, the round-up value of the correlation coefficient is 0.48, meaning that there is a relatively weak relationship between the two variables. The value of the coefficient of determination is 0.24, meaning that a linear relationship can explain 24% of the total variation in the number of HCIA instances.

Chart 9: The Irish relationship between the number of IHCIA instances and ICT performance indicators.

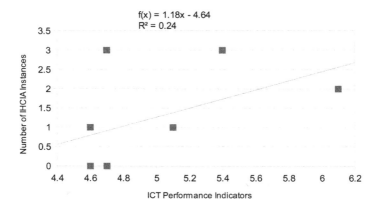

5 RESULTS

5.1 Results from the Descriptive Analysis

From Chart 4, which compares the two countries in terms of the number of IHCIA instances, it is possible to see that Finland has a higher number of instances. Chart 5 illustrates some similarities and differences between the two countries performance: commonality with regard to IHCIA instances of organizational support; availability and use of assistive technology; the presence of special legislation, policies; processes; and systems; the existence of measures taken in favor of accessibility; and the obligation to mark medicine packages with braille text for VIP are visible. Instances such as making internet resources available, demographic consideration during system design, and economic support for internet accessibility are, however, characteristics that are peculiar to the Finnish state, while educational IHCIA are peculiar to the data obtained from the Irish. In this comparison, Finland has eight existing IHCIA instances while Ireland has six of the instances from the total of nine. This result encouraged the author to look for more evidence, further analyzing the data on each country's performance in terms of ICT.

Using the data from Table 10 with the aim of finding which country has the better ICT performance, a descriptive analysis was made and Chart 6 was produced. The chart illustrates a comparison between the two countries in terms of the ICT performance indicator values. In the chart, it is possible to deduce that Finland had a better ICT performance in 2014. This might have significance for the purpose of studying whether there are any relationship between the ICT performance of a country and obtaining a higher number of IHCIA instances.

5.2 Results from the Regression Analysis

5.2.1 Results on the overall data analysis

The Regression analysis output for the overall relationship between the number of IHCIA instances and the ICT performance of both countries is shown in Tables 14.1 and 14.2. A slope of 2.04, a degree of freedom numerator (Dfn) of 1, a degree of freedom denominator (Dfd) of 6, and a probability (P-value) of 0.18 is seen.

Table 14.1: The best fit values with 95% confidence regression output for the overall relationship between number of IHCIA instances and ICT performance indicators.

Best fit values		95% confidence interval	Goodness of fit	
Slope	2.04 ± 1.35	-1.27 to 5.35	R^2	0.27
Y-intercept	-8.27 ± 7.34	-26.24 to 9.69	R	0.52
X-intercept	4.06	-infinity to 4.99	Standard deviation of residuals	1.54

Table 14.2: Slope significance and data regression output for the overall relationship between the number of IHCIA instances and ICT performance indicators.

Is slope significantly non-zero		Data	
F	2.27	XandY pairs	8
Dfn, Dfd	1,6	Equation	$f(X)=2.04X-8.27$
P-Value (F>2.27 or F<2.27)	0.18		
Deviation from horizontal	Not significant		

5.2.2 Finland data analysis results

The regression analysis output for the Finnish relationship between the number of IHCIA instances and ICT performance indicators is shown in Tables 15.1 and 15.2. This shows a slope of 1.44, a *Dfn* of 1, a *Dfd* of 6, and a *P-value* of 0.51.

Table 15.1: Best fit values with 95% confidence regression output analysis for the Finnish relationship between the two variables.

Best fit values		95% confidence interval	Goodness of fit	
Slope	1.44 ± 2.03	-3.53 to 6.41	R^2	0.08
Y-intercept	-5.33 ± 11.99	-34.68 to 24.01	R	0.28
X-intercept	3.71	-infinity to 5.60	Standard Deviation residuals	2.69

Table 15.2: Slope significance and data regression output analysis for the Finnish relationship between the two variables.

Is slope significantly non-zero		Data	
F	0.5	XandY pairs	8
Dfn, Dfd	1,6	Equation	$f(X)=1.44X-5.33$
P-Value(F>0.5 or F<0.5)	0.51		
Deviation from horizontal	Not Significant		

5.2.3 Ireland data analysis results

The Irish relationship between the number of IHCIA instances and ICT performance indicators is shown in Table 16.1 and 16.2. This shows a slope of 1.18, a *Dfn* of 1, a *Dfd* of 6, and a *P-value* of 0.22.

Table 16.1: Best fit values with 95% confidence for the Irish relationship between the two variables.

Best fit values		95% confidence interval	Goodness of fit	
Slope	1.18±0.86	-0.93 to 3.29	R^2	0.24
Y-intercept	-4.64±4.32	-15.20 to 5.92	R	0.49
X-intercept	3.93	-infinity to 4.85	Standard deviation of residuals	1.21

Table 16.2: Slope significance and data for the Irish relationship between the two variables.

Is slope significantly non-zero		Data	
F	1.88	XandY pairs	8
Dfn, Dfd	1,6	Equation	$f(X)=1.18X-4.64$
P-Value(F>1.88 or F<1.88)	0.22		
Deviation from horizontal	Not Significant		

6 DISCUSSION

6.1 The Core Basis

The simple comparison between the two countries in terms of the number of IHCIA instances is shown in Chart 4. From the chart, it can be seen that Finland has the higher number of IHCIA instances. Additionally, based on Chart 5 of the data analysis and the result section explaining it, Finland has eight existing IHCIA instances while Ireland has six of the instances from the total of nine. Here, the comparison was only made in terms of the existence or absence of instances. Based on the results thus far, Finland possesses a more socially inclusive HCIS. This is based on the assumption that a higher number of IHCIA is an indication of efforts to fulfill the healthcare information needs of VIP.

Nonetheless, other issues also need to be addressed such as the social, technological, financial or economic, and legal factors contributing to the awareness, accessibility, and motivational barriers within the context of IS. The study has tried to reveal the relationship between ICT and the HCI needs of the visually impaired. The overall indicator values, which themselves are categorized into the four factors after identifying the nature of their impact. For instance, ICT use and government efficiency has a social effect, accessibility of digital content has a technological effect, laws relating to ICTs have a legal effect, and the impact of ICTs on new services and products have an economic impact.

A comparison in terms of these performance values was made between the two countries. The results in Chart 6 shows that Finland has a better performance in terms of ICT. This led the researcher to look into the case more deeply to find if there is a relationship between the indicator values and having a higher number of IHCIA instances. According to this study, these are a measure for possessing more socially inclusive healthcare information systems and having more effective ICT systems. It is seen that Finland has more effective ICT systems established than Ireland and has a more socially inclusive healthcare information system. Does this mean that advances in ICT and fulfilling the healthcare information needs of the visually impaired are directly proportional? If so, then the hypothesis: "with the staggering advances in ICT in today's world, particularly in the most developed parts of the world such as Europe, the healthcare information needs of VIP are not being met" should be rejected. However, one can not reach such a conclusion on assumptions and based only on descriptive evidence derived from a relatively small sample. Strong evidence must be produced first by further analysis; there is also a need to collect more data in the future. Inferential analysis was used to further analyze the data collected and find stronger evidence of whether ICT and fulfilling the HCI needs of the visually impaired are directly proportional.

The result from the descriptive analysis might have significant value for the purpose of studying whether or not there is a relationship between the ICT performance of a country and obtaining a higher number of IHCIA instances. With this in mind, the alternative hypothesis can be tested using the statistical procedure. The alternative hypothesis depicted by *Ha* is stated as: "with the staggering advances in ICT in today's world, particularly in the most developed parts of the world such as Europe, the healthcare information needs of VIP are being met". Nonetheless, the current assumption of the null hypothesis, depicted by *Ho*, is that despite the staggering advances in ICT in today's world, even in the most developed parts of the world such as Europe, the healthcare information needs of VIP are not being met. *Ha* is suggesting a strong and positive relationship between the dependent and independent variables. In other words, for every advancement in ICT in the developed regions of Europe, there are significant gains in terms of fulfilling the HCI needs of VIP. This can perhaps be interpreted as meaning that having greater ICT performance indicator values is directly proportional to having a higher number of IHCIA instances. The process of hypothesis testing that checks whether the claim is a plausible explanation of the experimental findings is presented as follows:

The Null hypothesis: *Ho* = "despite the staggering advances in ICT in today's world, even in the most developed parts of the world such as Europe, the healthcare information needs of VIP are not being met"

Therefore:

$The_{assumption} = Ho : \beta 1 = 0, where \beta 1 is the slope, other condition : R is close 0$

Alternative hypothesis: *Ha* = "with the staggering advances in ICT in today's world, particularly in the most developed parts of the world such as Europe, the healthcare information needs of VIP are being met"

Therefore:

$The_{claim} = Ha : \beta 1 ! = 0, \beta 1 is the slope, Other condition : 0.5 < R \leq 1$

Now, the assumption or null hypothesis neither suggests that when there are advances in ICT, the healthcare information needs of the visually impaired are being left out or ignored, nor does it suggest that fulfilling the HCI needs of visually impaired is directly proportional to the advancement in ICT. It simply states that advances in ICT are neither directly proportional nor inversely proportional to the fulfillment of the HCI needs of VIP. It claims that there is a weak and non-linear relationship between the two variables. In this type of scenario, a two-tailed test is appropriate. To do this simply, first, let the level of confidence be 95%; c is then the probability value for the level of confidence, which in this case is 0.95, thus making the level of significance for α to be 0.05, which is obtained using the formula 1 minus c. The values of α, *p-value*, and R are important to reach a sound conclusion.

Second, a linear regression test will determine whether to accept or reject *Ho*. This study interprets values obtained as a weight of evidence against *Ho* as part of a decision rule for rejection. Table 17 below shows the risk analysis to prevent errors, namely Type I and Type II, from occurring when making a decision about the validity of *Ho*. Type I errors occur when the researcher rejects a true hypothesis, and Type II error occur when the researcher accepts a false hypothesis. A Type II error simply implies that there is a lack of strong evidence from the data collected to claim *Ho* is false. The probability of a Type II error is is denoted by β. The probability of correctly rejecting a false *Ho* is called power and is calculated from the formula 1 minus β.

Table 17: Risk analysis table to prevent wrong conclusions.

Current perceived reality	Conclusion based on the research finding	
	Ho Is False	*Ho* Is True
Ho Is True	Type I error	Valid
Ho Is False	Valid	Type II error

Third, for each case, the *p-value* is obtained using the F-distribution calculator to assess the cumulative probability associated with an *F-value*. Additionally, their *R-value* is used to explain the strength of the relationship between the dependent and independent variables. Finally, this is followed by findings in order to accept or reject the null hypothesis. However, in this case, the study has chosen to use the *p-* and *R-values* as an indication of the weight of evidence rather than using it as a decision rule for rejection. The process simply compares the *p-value* with the significance level, questions the alternative hypothesis, and favors the null hypothesis as the *p-value* is less than α and the *R-value* is less than 0.5.

6.2 The Overall Relationship

Findings based on the regression output for the overall relationship between the number of IHCIA instances and ICT performance indicators are shown in Table 14 of section 5.2.1 and Chart 7 of section 4.3.2. The cumulative probability of the F-statistic (*p-value*) of a two-tailed test with an F-statistic value of 2.27 is calculated using the following two steps:

Step 1: $p(cumulative)=p(F<2.27)+p(F>2.27)$

Step 2: $p(cumulative)=2*(1-(p(F\leq2.27)))$

Computing the following values using a value of 1 for the given degrees of freedom numerator (*Dfn*) and a value of 6 for the degrees of freedom denominator (*Dfd*) (or the number of observations), gives a cumulative *p-value* of 0.36. The critical value at an α of 0.05 for the given *Dfn* of 1 and *Dfd* of 6 is 5.9874, whilst the F-test result reads 0.36, which is less than the critical value. Consequently, the researcher failed to reject the null hypothesis. Additionally, the *R-value*, namely the correlation coefficient, has a calculated value of 0.52, which suggests a relatively weak relationship between the two variables. Finally, the calculated value of the coefficient of determination or R^2 is 0.27. In other words, a linear relationship between the two variables with the formula $f(X)=2.04X-8.27$ can explain 27% of the total variation in the dependent variable, whilst it fails to explain the other 73%.

6.3 Finland

Using the same procedure for the same values of *Dfn* and *Dfd*, but with an F-statistic value of 0.5, gives a cumulative *p-value* of 1.02. The critical value at α of 0.05 for the given *Dfn* of 1 and *Dfd* of 6 is 5.9874, whilst the F-test result reads 1.02, which is less than the critical value. Thus, the researcher also failed to reject the null hypothesis for the Finnish case. Furthermore, the *R-value* is 0.28, which is interpreted as a very weak relationship between the two variables. Finally, R^2 is 0.08, meaning that a linear relationship between the two variables with the formula $f(X)=1.44X-5.33$ can explain only 8% of the total variation in the dependent variable, whilst it fails to explain 92% of the total variation.

6.4 Ireland

For the final case, using the same procedure for the same values of *Dfn* and *Dfd*, but with an F-statistic value of 1.88 or $P(F\leq1.88)$ of 0.78. Since this is a two-tailed test, the formula $P(F<1.88)+P(F>1.88)$ gives a cumulative *p-value* of 0.44. The critical value at α of 0.05 for the given *Dfn* of 1 and *Dfd* of 6 is 5.9874, whilst the F-test result reads 0.44, which is less than the critical value. Thus, the researcher failed to reject the null hypothesis in the Irish case. Additionally, the *R-value* is 0.49 depicting a weak relationship between the two variables. In this case, the dependent variable is the number of IHCIA and the independent variable is ICT performance indicators. Finally, R^2 is 0.24, which indicates that a linear relationship between the two variables with the formula $f(X)=1.18X-4.64$ can explain 24% of the total variation in the dependent variable, whilst it fails to explain 76% of the total variation in the number of IHCIA.

The *p-values* of all of the three F-statistic values are less than the critical value of the F-distribution value at a significance level 0.05 of 5.9874. Therefore, there is a lack of evidence to reject the null hypothesis. Furthermore, the correlation coefficient R and the coefficient of determination R^2 values of the three cases are less than 0.5. Here, coefficient values that are less than 0.5 are interpreted as "weak but positive" and "a poor representation of the data by regression line", respectively.

7 CONCLUSIONS

There are already laws in place, policies designed, and existing procedures and guidelines that supervise the provision of the healthcare information (HCI) needs of visually impaired people (VIP). Everyone has the right to information as it is a fundamental human right. Hence, VIP must get information that is timely, that is in an accessible format, and that has a high degree of relevance and use. At the moment, there are barriers posing difficulties to the delivery of healthcare information to VIP, and as a result the HCI needs of these individuals are not yet fulfilled.

According to this study, the major types of healthcare information access barriers can be categorized as awareness, accessibility, and motivational barriers. The major factors identified that are involved in the creation of barriers are social, technological, financial or economic, and legal. Visual impairment is, nevertheless, the root cause of the digital disability divide and has a negative effect on information accessibility. Its effect, however, can be mitigated with the proper planning, designing, development, and implementation of healthcare service processes with advanced ICTs, while taking into account user diversity, the different types of technology, and the gaps in user knowledge. Patient participation in the planning phase will help to avoid inadequate developments and at the same time facilitate innovation.

Currently, the digital divide is significant, and there are not enough governmental or social incentives to minimize the VID3 effect in Europe. Although visual impairment itself is the major source of the digital divide, with the great advances in ICT, the digital divide can be eventually bridged and increased social inclusion will be realized. The achievement of a special healthcare information system (HCIS) comprised of advanced technologies could be expensive to implement. However, once successfully implemented, it will serve as a healthcare information source capable of providing HCI with the patient's choice of accessible formats. For example, a combination of assistive technologies for input, back-end, and output produced using universal design principles can be put together to create logical ISs that will empower VIP and enable them to access the available HCI. This, in turn, will increase social inclusion whilst this helping to remove the communication barriers and thus bridging the VID3.

This study shares the view of a number of scholars that advances in ICT in today's world are intensifying social exclusion and the inefficient and the non-visually impaired people inclusive HCIS is among the outputs thereof. The null hypothesis of this study shared the same thought and there was not enough evidence produced to reject it. Therefore, the conclusion of this study is in favor of this notion.

8 RECOMMENDATIONS

ICT can surely impact positively on the healthcare information and the Internet provision of the visually impaired. New developments in technology should take the needs of these individuals into consideration. Nevertheless, not only does this group have difficulty accessing their healthcare information, they are also profoundly disconnected from all manner of social activities. This is especially true in this digital era, where everyday living is becoming dependent on cyber-space. This should be an opportune moment to use these technical gains to help VIP to lead an independent life. This individual's right to information, privacy, and confidentiality must be respected and in each of case, the ability to lead independent life plays an important role.

Healthcare information is important for VIP to lead a high quality and healthy life. ICT devices, assistive software applications, and the Web together with the Internet are the major components of technology that need serious intervention to make them suitable for the visually impaired people and to eradicate the VID3. The use of assistive technologies can play an important role in delivering an alternative format to the patient. However, it is vital to remember that the visually impaired are a heterogeneous group and the appropriate types of assistive technologies and output formats will vary according to the severity of vision loss.

Inclusion in production in all fields of technological design, development, and production is also relevant. The visually impaired should be allowed to participate in technological designs that are intended to fill gaps in HCI accessibility. Thus, technology manufacturers must stop the unintentional marginalization and segregation caused by their mass production of ICT devices. They need to find new ways to make products with good usability accessible to the visually impaired. They may, for example, consider Design for All principles during production. Once such devices are produced, their affordability and availability must be checked as most of the assistive technologies in the market are expensive.

It is very important to consider educational incentives that aim to increase the knowledge and skills of VIP. Facilitating social innovations that aim to ease employment conditions also impact positively on VIP purchasing power and their attitude towards using technology, which in turn increases motivation. Healthcare providers must be informed about the rights and special HCI needs of the visually impaired. Executives must know their role and act accordingly as they are required to plan, direct, and coordinate healthcare services for the visually impaired as well. Blind institutes must truly act as advocates for people with disadvantages and participate actively in research such as this.

In general, efforts to alleviate the VID3 effect could begin with the coordination of public health activities, increasing the availability of eye care services, and raising awareness about accessible medical treatments for treatable visual impairments. In more detail, one can follow four major steps to accomplish this.

First, a consensus must be reached among visually impaired patients, healthcare executives, healthcare providers, and manufacturers about the need for special and intelligent design, development, and production of HCI devices that are capable of minimizing social exclusion while increasing inclusion in production.

Second, action must be taken to avoid accessibility barriers by adopting new ICT technologies, such as assistive technologies, that can increase visually impaired patients participation.

Third, a method that diminishes motivational barriers must be invoked. This can be done by arranging purpose-driven education sessions that aim to boost VIP motivation towards the use of technology.

Fourth, a detailed study about technological, legal, financial, and social factors within an ICT context must be conducted. This should be followed by a similar study on the accessibility of healthcare information while being affected by the identified ICT factors that can create information provision barriers.

Finally, to reverse the thinking on the healthcare information access barriers, which are illustrated in Figure 1, and design a sound framework to be used when developing a healthcare information system that is capable of encompassing all in terms of delivering services.

Countries must have IHCIA for the visually impaired. These incentives must be systematic so as to bring about a real change by considering the barriers and the associated factors involved in their creation. ICT injected healthcare information incentives, such as the availability of special healthcare information internet resources and assistive technologies, are directly proportional to the ICT capabilities of a country.

Therefore, a further study is needed to identify the relationship between ICT performance indicators and IHCIA. The next study should aim to categorize these ICT performance indicators into the respective factors that contribute to HCIA barriers in the context of IS. This should be followed by the acquisition of large data sets to perform multivariate regression statistical analysis. The findings from such research could help reveal what is needed to achieve a more socially inclusive HCIS. The apotheosis of technology's design and production will be known by its capability to enable the widest variety of disabled users to perform their daily tasks with little or no help from outside parties.

REFERENCES

Adam, A. - Kreps, D. (2006) Social Inclusion: Societal and Organizational Implications for Information Systems. In Trauth, E. - Howcroft, D. - Butler, T. - Fitzgerald, DeGross, B. - Boston, J. (eds.), *International Federation for Information Processing (IFIP)*, Vol. 208, 217-228.

American Association of Deaf-Blind (AADB). (2009). How do deaf-blind people communicate? 2009. Available at: http://www.aadb.org/factsheets/db_communicat ions.html (Accessed 30.09.2016)

American Council of the Blind (ACB). (2016). Our Mission 2016. Available at: http://www.acb.org/ (Accessed 20.10.2016)

American Foundation for the Blind (AFB). (2016). Population and Demographic Sttistics for Adults who are Blind or Visually Impaired 2015. Available at: http://www.afb.org/info/blindness-statistics/research-navigator-just-how-many-blind-folks-are-there-anyway/25 (Accessed 20.10.2016)

Ando, B. - Baglio, S. - La Malfa, S. - Marletta, V. (2011) A sensing architecture for mutual user-environment awareness case of study: a mobility aid for the visually impaired. *IEEE Sensors Journal*, Vol. 11(3), 634-640.

Beverley, C. A. - Bath, P. A. - Barber, R. (2007) Can two established information models explain the information behaviour of visually impaired people seeking health and social care information?. *Journal of Documentation*, Vol. 63, 9-32.

Beverley, C. A. - Bath, P. A. - Barber, R. (2011) Health and social care information for legally blind people. *Aslib Proceedings*, Uk, Vol. 63(2/3), 256-274.

Borg, J. - Larsson, S. - Östergren, P. (2011a) The right to assistive technology: for whom, for what, and by whom?. *Disability and Society*, 151-167, DOI: 10.1080/09687599.2011.543862.

Borg, J. - Lindström, A. - Larsson, S. (2011b) Assistive technology in developing countries: a review from the perspective of the Convention on the Rights of Persons with Disabilities. *The International Society for Prosthetics and Orthotics*, Vol. 35, 20-29.

British Medical Association (BMA). (2007) Disability equality within healthcare: The role of healthcare professionals. *BMA equal opportunities committee and patient liaison group*, 1-48.

Bucy, E. P. (2000) Social access to the Internet. *The Harvard International Journal of Press/Politics*, Vol. 5, 50-61.

Centers for Disease Control and Prevention (CDC). (2016). The Burden of Vision Loss, Population Estimates 2009. Avaliable at: http://www.cdc.gov/visionhealth/basic _information/vision_loss_burden.htm (Accessed 20.10.2016)

66

Citizens Information. (2016). Employment rights of people with disabilities 2016. Available at: http://www.citizensinformation.ie/en/employment/employment_and_disability/working_with_a_disability.html (Accessed 10.10.2016)

Coffey, M. - Coufopoulos, A. - Kinghorn, K. (2014) Barriers to employment for visually impaired women. *International Journal of Workplace Health Management*, Vol. 7, 171-185.

Cooper, M. - Sloan, D. - Kelly, B. - Lewthwaite, S. (2012) Achallenge to Web Accessibility Meterics and Guidelines: Putting People and Processes First. In: *W4A 2012: 9th International Cross-Disciplinary Conference on Web Accessibility*, 1-4, DOI: 10.1145/2207016.2207028.

Crawford, M. J. - Rutter, D. - Manley, C. - Weaver, T. - Bhui, K. - Fulop, N. - Tyrer, P. (2002) Systematic review of involving patients in the planning and development of healt care. *British Mediacal Journal (BMJ)*, Vol. 325, 1-5.

Cullen, R. (2001) Addressing the digital divide. *Online Information Review*, Vol. 25, 311-320.

Cupples, M. P. - Hart, P M. - Jackson, A. J. (2012) Improving healthcare access for people with visual impairment and blindness. *Clinical Review*, Department of General Practice, Queen's University, Belfast; Belfast Health and Social Care Trust, Belfast; Royal National Institute for the Blind, Belfast; Australian College of Optometry, Melbourne, Australia, 1-5.

DAISY Suomen DAISY konsortio. (2016). The Finnish DAISY Consortium 2016. Available at https://www.daisy-konsortio.fi/finnish-daisy-consortium/ (Accessed 1-5.10.2016)

Deutscher Blinden-und Sehbehindertenverband (DBSV). (2016). Federation of the Blind and Visually Impaired of France (FAF) 2016. Available at: http://www.comenius-eveil.eu/index.phpmenuid=29andreporeid=23andgetlang=fr (Accessed 17.-10.2016)

Disabled Access Day. (2016). Accessible formats 2016. Available at: http://www.disabledaccessday.com/news/accessible-formats/ (Accessed 3.10.2016)

Dr. Holdings, F. (2009) RNIB Health information for blind and partially sighted people: Senior Research Executive. London, The United Kingdom: The Information Centre for Health and Social care and Dr Foster Intelligence.

Dr. Jacob, P. D. (2008) The Enterprise of Healthcare: Clinical Information Systems an Overview July 2008. Avaliable at: http://ehealth.eletsonline.com/2008/07/11156/ (Accessed 13.07.2016)

EuroBlind. (2016a). Information for countries, United Kingdom. National implementation and monitoring - Article 33 2014. Available at: http://www.euroblind.org/convention/article-33--national-implementation-and-monitoring/nr/2168 (Accessed 10.10.2016)

EuroBlind. (2016b). Information for countries, France. National implementation and monitoring Article 33 2014. Available at: http://www.euroblind.org/convention/ar ticle-33—national-implementation-and-monitoring/nr/2100 (Accessed10.10.2016)

European Commission. (2015). Employment Social Affairs and Inclusion 2015. Available at: http://ec.europa.eu/social/main.jsp?catId=1189andlangId=en (Accessed 12.10.2016)

European Union Agency For Fundamental Rights (FRA). (2016). EU Framework for the UN Convention on the Rights of Persons with Disabilities 2016. Available at: http://fra.europa.eu/en/theme/people-disabilities/eu-crpd-framework (Accessed 12.10.2016)

FIMEA. (2015). Marketing Authorisations. Braille and package leaflets for the visually impaired 2015. Available at: http://www.fimea.fi/web/en/marketing_authorisati ons/product_information/Braille_and_package_leaflets_for_the_visually_impaired (Accessed 15.10.2016)

Finnish Federation of Visually Impaired (FFVI) (2012). Strategic objectives and measures of the Federal Assembly for the period 2012-2016 (Strategiset tavoitteet ja toimenpiteet liittokokouskaudelle 2012–2016) 2012. Available at: http://www.nkl.fi/fi/etusivu/nkl_ry/strategia/7478 (Accessed 15.10.2016)

Finnish Federation of Visually Impaired (FFVI). (2016). Visual Impairment in Finland. July 2016. Available at: http://nkl.fi/7/english (Accessed 17.07.2016)

Frances, M. - D'Andrea - Siu, Yue-Ting. (2015) Students with Visual Impairments: Considerations and Effective Practices for Technology Use. In Dave L. Edyburn (ed.), *Efficacy of Assistive Technology Interventions*, Vol. 1, 111-138.

Green, D. - Ducorroy, G. - McElnea, E. - Naughton, A. - Skelly, A. - O'Neill, C. - Kenny, D. - Keegan, D. (2016) The Cost of Blindness in the Republic of Ireland 2010-2020. *Journal of Ophthalmology*, Hindawi Publishing Corporation, 1-8.

Gunter, T. D - Terry, N. P. (2005). The Emergence of National Electronic Health Record Architectures in the United States and Australia: Models, Costs, and Questions. *Journal of Medical Internet Research*. 20057(1):e3., DOI: 10.2196/jmir.7.1.e3.

HealthIT.gov. (2015). Office of the National Coordinator for Health IT: What are the differences between electronic medical records, electronic health records, and personal health records? 2015. Avaliable at: https://www.healthit.gov/providers-professionals/faqs/what-are-differences-between-electronic-medical-recordselec tronic (Accessed 13.07.2016)

Health Service Executive (HSE). (2016). National Guidelines on Accessible Health and Social Care Services: Part Two. You and Your Health Service 2016. Available at: http://www.hse.ie/eng/services/yourhealthservice/access/NatGuideAccessibleServices/part2.html (Accessed 19.10.2016)

Hindman, D. B. (2000) The rural-urban digital divide. *Journalism and Mass Communication Quarterly*, 77, 549–560.

Hoffman, D. - Novak, T. - Scholsser, A. (2000) The Evolution of the Digital Divide: How Gaps in Internet Access May Impact Electronic Commerce. *Owen Graduate School of Management Vanderbilt University*, 1-55.

Human Factors and Ergonomics Society (HFES). (2008). ANSI/HFES 200 Human Factors Engineering of Software User Interfaces 2008. Available at: http://www.hfes.org/Publications/ProductDetail.aspx?Id=76 (Accessed 12.08.2016)

Inclusion Ireland. (2016). The United Nations and Disability. Available at: http://www.inclusionireland.ie/content/page/united-nations-and-disability (Accessed 10.10.2016)

Index Braille Pricing. (2016). Braille Embosser Manufacturer. Available at: http://www.indexBraille.com/en-us/sales/pricing?c=EUR 2016 (Accessed 30.09.2016)

Informing Families of Their Child's Disability. (2016). Appropriate, Accurate Information. National Council for the Blind of Ireland (NCBI) 2016. Available at: http://-www.informingfamilies.ie/a-z-of-supports-and-information/nationalcouncil for the blind-of-ireland-ncbi.316.html (Accessed 18.10.2016)

Jhangianti, I. (2006) Usability and Accessibility Issues in the Localization of Assistive Technology. *Proceedings of the 8th international ACM SIGACCESS conference on Computers and accessibility*, 299-300, DOI: 10.1145/1168987.1169065.

Jones, S. - Johnson-Yale, C. - Millermaier, S. - Perez, F. S. (2009) U.S. college students' Internet use: Race, gender and digital divides. *Journal of Computer mediated Communication*, Vol. 14, 244-264, DOI: 10.1111/j.1083-6101.2009.01439.x.

Kane, S. K. - Jayant, C. - Wobbrock, J. O. - Ladner, R. E. (2009). Freedom to roam: A study of mobile device adoption and accessibility for people with visual and motor disabilities. *In ASSETS'09 - Proceedings of the 11th International ACM SIGACCESS Conference on Computers and Accessibility*, 115-122, DOI: 10.1145/1639642.1639663.

Kelly, S. M. - Clark-Bischke, C. (2011) Chapter 9 History of visual impairments: in Rotatori, A.F. - Obiakor, F. E. - Bakken, J. P (ed.) *History of Special Education (Advances in Special Education, Vol. 21).* Emerald Group Publishing Limited, 213-236.

Kleynhans, S. A - Fourie, I. (2014) Ensuring accessibility of electronic information resources for visually impaired people: The need to clarify concepts such as visually impaired. *Library Hi Tech*, Vol. 32, 368-379.

Kolibre. (2016). What is Kolibre?. Organisation 2016. Available at: http://www.kolibr e.org/en/organization (Accessed 5.10.2016)

Kumar, S. - Sanaman, G. (2015) Web challenges faced by blind and vision impaired users in libraries of Delhi. *The Electronic Library*, Vol. 33, 242-257.

Li, J. (2010) Developing accessible e-learning content. *Paper presented at 2nd International Conference on Information Science and Engineering (ICISE)*, DOI: 10.1109/ICISE.2010.5690170.

Living Made Easy. (2016). Braille Keyboards. Clear, Practical Advice on Daily Living Equipment 2016. Available at: http://www.livingmadeeasy.org.uk/communicati on/Braille-keyboards-2962-p/ (Accessed 20.09.2016)

Loges, W. E – Jung, Joo-Young (2001) Exploring the digital divide: Internet connecte-dness and age. *Communication Research*, Vol. 28 (4), 536-562, DOI: 10.1177/0 09365001028004007.

Longford Leader. (2017). Government has 'no respect whatsoever' for people with disa-bilities 2017. Available at: http://www.longfordleader.ie/news/features/233836/ government-has-no-respect-whatsoever-for-people-with-disabilities.html (Acce-ssed 05.02.2017)

Mavrou, K. (2011) Assistive technology as an emerging policy and practice: processes, challenges and future directions. *Technology and Disability*, Vol. 23 (1), 41-52, DOI: 10.3233/TAD-2011-0311.

McAuliffe, E. (2014) Clinical governance in the Irish health system: a review of progress. *Clinical Governance.* Vol. 19, 296-313.

Ministry of Social Affairs and Health (MSAH). (2016). Services and support for people with disabilities 2016. Available at: http://stm.fi/en/disability-services (Accessed 15.10.2016)

Minnesota Department of Human Services (DHS). (2016). Accessible Formats 2011. A-vailable at: http://www.dhs.state.mn.us/main/idcplgIdcService=GET_DYNAMI C_CONVERSIONandRevisionSelectionMethod=LatestReleasedanddDocName =dhs16_164569 (Accessed 3.10.2016)

National Disability Authority (NDA). (2016). About us. 2016. Available at: http://nda.i e/About-us/ (Accessed 19.10.2016)

National Federation of Blind (NFB). (2016). Technology Resource List. Available at: https://nfb.org/technology-resource-list#BTSoftware (Accessed 30.09.2016)

National Health Service (NHS). (2016). Health and high quality care for all, now and f-or future generations 2016. Accessible Information Standard. Making health and social care information accessible. July 2016. Avaliable at: https://www.englan-d.nhs.uk/ourwork/accessibleinfo/ (Accessed 16.10.2016)

NOLO. (2016). Blind and Low Vision Persons' Right to Health Care Information in Alternative Formats 2016. Available at: http://www.nolo.com/legalencyclopedia/blind-low-vision-persons-right-health-care-information-alternative-formats.html (Accessed 20.10.2016)

O'Herlihy Access Consultancy (OHAC). (2016). About us 2016. Available at: http://www.accessconsultancy.ie/about (Accessed 18.10.2016)

Ojamo, M. - Uusitalo, H. (2012) The Finnish Register of Visual Impairment. Annual Statistics. Helsinki, Finland: The National Institute for Health and Welfare (THL) and Näkövammaisten kirjastoyhdistys ry (The Library Association of the Visually Impaired).

OPC. (2016). Preserver La Vue. Visual Impairment 2016. Available at: http://www.opc.asso.fr/?Visual-Impairment,830andlang=fr/ (Accessed 17.10.2016)

Pal, J. - Pradhan, P. - Shah, M. - Babu, R. (2011) Assistive Technology for Vision impairments: An Agenda for the ICTD Community. *The International World Wide Web Conference Committee (IW3C2)*, 513-522.

Perkins School For Blind. (2016). Braille Displays. Assitive Technology Store 2016. Available at: http://www.perkinsproducts.org/store/en/39-Braille-displays (Accessed 30.09.2016)

Public Health France. (2013). INPES. Accessibility to health information for people with disabilities 2013. Available at: http://inpes.santepubliquefrance.fr/30000/actus2013/025-accessibilite-information.asp (Accessed 17.10.2016)

Queen's University. (2008). Accessibility Hub 2008. Available at: http://www.queens-u.ca/accessibility/how-info/what-are-alternate-formats (Accessed 5.10.2016)

Rice, R. - Haythornthwaite, C. (2006) Perspectives on Internet use: access, involvement and interaction in L. Lievrouw and S. Livingstone (eds.), *Handbook of new media: Social shaping and consequences of ICTs (student edn)*, London: Sage, 92–113.

Royal National Institute of Blind (RNIB). (2014a). How many people in the UK have sight loss? 2014. Available at: https://help.rnib.org.uk/help/newly-diagnosed-registration/registering-sight-loss/statistics (Accessed 21.07.2016)

Royal National Institute of Blind People (RNIB). (2016). Supporting People With Sight Loss. History of RNIB 2016. Available at: http://www.rnib.org.uk/about-rnib-who-we-are/history-rnib (Accessed 16.10.2016)

Royal National Institute of Blind People (RNIB). (2014b). Supporting People With Sight Loss. Making NHS information accessible 2014. Available at: http://www.rnib.org.uk/making-nhs-information-accessible (Accessed 16.10.2016)

Sachdeva, N. – Tuikka, AM. – Kimppa, KK. - Suomi, R. (2015) Digital disability divide in information society A framework based on a structured literature review. *Journal of University of Turku, Finland*, Vol. 13 (3/4), 283-298.

Sachdeva, N. – Tuikka, AM. – Suomi, R. (2013) Digital disability divide in information society: the case of impairments. *Proceedings of the Possibilities of Ethical IT Conference, University of Southern Denmark, Kolding*, 405-412.

Sapp, W. (2003) Visual impairment: In Effective Education for Learners with Exceptionalities. *Elsevier Science Limited*, Vol. 15, 259-282.

Saulo, B. - Walakira, E. - Darj, E. (2011) Access to healthcare for disabled persons: How are blind people reached by HIV services?. *Sexual and Reproductive Healthcare*, Vol. 3, 49-53.

Sharby, N. - Martire, K. - Iversen, M. D. (2015). Decreasing Health Disparities for People with Disabilities through Improved Communication Strategies and Awareness 2015. *International Journal of Environmental Research and Public Health*, Vol. 12, 3301-3316.

Schiemer, M. - Proyer, M. (2013) Teaching children with disabilities: ICTs in Bangkok and Addis Ababa. *Multicultural Education and Technology Journal*, Vol. 7, 99-112.

Social Inclusion. (2016). Social Portrait of People with Disabilities in Ireland 2011. Available at: http://socialinclusion.ie/publications/SocialPortraitDisabilities.html (-Accessed 10.10.2016)

The French Confederation for the Welfare of the Blind and Partially Sighted (Confédération Française pour la Promotion Sociale des Aveugles et: Amblyopes (CFPS-AA)) 2016. Available at: http://www.cfpsaa.fr/ (Accessed 11.10.2016)

The Irish Times. (2016a). Budget 2017 needs to tackle disability issues. Available at: http://www.irishtimes.com/opinion/budget-2017-needs-to-tackle-disability-issues-1.2819529 (Accessed 06.02.2017).

The Irish Times. (2016b). UN convention on disabilities will be ratified, says Finian McGrath. Available at: http://www.irishtimes.com/news/social-affairs/unconvention-on-disabilities-will-be-ratified-says-finian-mcgrath-1.2641487 (Accessed 06-.02.2017).

The Ministy for Foreign Affairs of Finland. (2016). Finland ratifies the Convention on the Rights of Persons with Disabilities and its Optional Protocol 2016. Available at: http://formin.finland.fi/public/default.aspx?contentid=346204 (Accessed 08.05.2016)

Uk Vision Strategy. (2014). Eye Health Data Summary. A review of published data in England 2014. Available at: http://www.rnib.org.uk/sites/default/files/Eye_health_data_summary_report_2014.pdf (Accessed 16.10.2016)

United Nations (UN). (2006). UN Web Services Section, Department of Public Information: Convention on The Rights of Persons with Disabilities 2006. Available at: http://www.un.org/disabilities/convention/conventionfull.shtml (Accessed 20.07.2016)

United Nations (UN). (2007). Accessibility. A guiding principle of the Convention 200 7. Available at: http://www.un.org/esa/socdev/enable/disacc.htm (Accessed 21. 07.2016)

United Nations Human Rights Office of The High Comissioner (OHCHR). (2016b).The right of persons with disabilities to social protection 2015. Available at: http://w ww.ohchr.org/EN/Issues/Disability/SRDisabilities/Pages/SocialProtection.aspx (Accessed 10.10.2016)

Usability Geek. (2016). 10 Free Screen Readers For Blind Or Visually Impaired Users. Available at: http://usabilitygeek.com/10-free-screen-reader-blind-visually-imp aired-users/ (Accessed 30.09.2016)

US National Library of Medicine. (2016). National Institutes of Health. Disability, sight impairment, and the law 2006. Available at: https://www.ncbi.nlm.nih.gov/pmc/ articles/PMC1857435/ (Accessed 10.10.2016)

U.S. Department of State Diplomacy in Action. (2016). The Disabilities Treaty: Openin g the World to Americans with Disabilities 2016. Available at: http://www.state .gov/j/drl/sadr/disabilitiestreaty/index.htm (Accessed 8.10.2016)

United Nations Human Rights Office of The High Comissioner (OHCHR). (2016a). Ar- ticle 19 of the International Covenant on Civil and Political Rights (ICCPR) 16 December 1966. Available at: http://www.ohchr.org/en/professionalinterest/pag es/ccpr.aspx (Accessed 20.07.2016)

Verick, S. (2004) Do financial incentives promote the employment of the disabled?. *IZ- A Discussion Paper No. 1256.* IZA Bonn and University of Bonn.

Vicente, M. R. - Lopez, A. J. (2010) A Multidimensional Analysis of the Disability Digital Divide: Some Evidence for Internet Use. *The Information Society An International Journal*, C, Vol. 26, 48-64.

Wahl, H. W. - Fänge, A. - Oswald, F. - Gitlin, L. N. - Iwarsson, S. (2009). The home environment and disability-related outcomes in aging individuals: What is the empirical evidence? *The Gerontologist*, Vol. 49 (3), 355–367.

Walsh, K. - Antony, J. (2007) Improving patient safety and quality. *International Journal of Health Care Quality Assurance*, Vol. 20, 107-115.

Wei, L. - Hindman, D. B. (2011) Does the digital divide matter more? Comparing the effects of new media and old media use on the education-based knowledge gap. *Mass Communication and Society*, Vol. 14 (2), 216–235.

Wei, L. - Zhang, M. (2008) The adoption and use of mobile phone in rural China: A case study of Hubei. China. *Telematics and Informatics*, Vol. 25 (3), 169-186.

Wills, C. - Moumtzi, V. - Vontas, A. (2010) A real case study of assistive living ecosystems. *2010 Fourth IEEE International Conference on Digital Ecosystems and Technologies (DEST)*, Dubai, 147-151.

Wilson, K. R. - Wallin, J. S, - Reiser, C. (2003) Social Stratification and the Digital Divide. *Social Science Computer Review*, Vol. 21 (2), 133-143.

World Economic Forum. (2014) The top 10 countries for embracing IT, ICT use and go vernment efficiency 2014. Available at: https://www.weforum.org/agenda/214/0 4/top-10-countries-embracing-information-technology/. Accessible online: http// :www3.weforum.org/docs/WEF_GlobalInformationTechnology_Report_2014.p df (Accessed 30.10.2016)

World Health Organization (WHO). (2016a). Media centre: Visual Impairment and Bli ndness August 2016. Available at: http://www.who.int/mediacentre/factsheets/f s282/en/ (Accessed 17.07.2016)

World Health Organization (WHO). (2016b). Prevention of Blindness and Visual Impairment: Global trends in the magnitude of blindness and visual impairment 2016. Available at: http://www.who.int/blindness/causes/trends/en/ (Accessed 21.07.-2016)

Yeo, R. - Moore, K. (2003) Including Disabled People in Poverty Reduction Work: "Nothing About Us, Without Us". *World Development*, Vol.31 (3), 571-590.

Zetterström, E. (2012). Identifying Barriers to Accessibility in Qatar. In K. Miesenberger, K. - Karshmer, A - Penaz, P. - Zagler, W. (eds.), *Computers Helping People with Special Needs*, Vol. 7382, 235-242.

APPENDICES

Appendix 1: Healthcare information needs of the Visually Impaired

1. Which are the most important Internet resources in your country that deliver health information with special arrangements for visually impaired?

Name of the service

URL

Name of the service

URL

Name of the service

URL

Name of the service

URL

2. Which are the most important companies/organizations in your country that deliver health information with special arrangements for visually impaired?

Name of the organization

URL

Name of the organization

URL

Name of the organization

URL

Name of the organization

3. Which are the most important assistive technologies such as speech software, scanners, and etc. put in place to help the visually impaired access healthcare information?

4. Which are the most important special legislations, policies, processes, or systems put in place to satisfy the healthcare information needs of the visually impaired in your country?

5. Which are the main education initiatives in your country to help visually impaired to get access to health information?

6. Do the policies, processes and systems designed take into account the different demographic conditions (i.e. Gender, Age, the severity of blindness, level of education, socio-economic groups, and geographic location) of the visually impaired? Which conditions have been taken well into consideration and which conditions are less well catered for?

7. Is it obligatory in your country to mark medicine packages with braille text?

8. Which are the economics support measures in your country to support Internet access of visually impaired citizen? Can you give links to any English-speaking material on this issue?

Support measure

URLSupport measure

URL

Support measure

URL

Support measure

URL

Support measure

9. Please report freely the most important measures in your country to support visually impaired in their access to health information?

10. Thank you for your participation! Please write us here if you have any additional remarks and please leave your e-mail if you wish to get the results of the survey!

APPENDIX 2: Cover letter for the survey

Fidsha Seyoum Teshome

Move all 48 replymails

Dear Recipient,

Visual Impairment is a major source of Digital Divide and a health risk in many aspects. Yet we know internationally very little about national arrangements to support visually impaired in their health information access. In order to tackle this problem, we have administered this survey. The main goal of the research is to find out national best practices to support visually impaired in their health information access.

Please support us and participate in the research by answering the questionnaire from the
link https://www.webropolsurveys.com. Answer Survey Participation.aspx?SID=Fm1075697&SID=82b4d0d-7f8e-4865-baf8-03715bcf2f02&dy=1401140010

You are very welcome to add any additional remarks, and you will get the results of the survey, if you leave your e-mail address to the last question of the survey.

We look forward to your answers by 20.3.2016.
Thank you in advance for your time and collaboration!

Reima Suomi   Fidsha Seyoum Teshome
Professor   Student
Information Systems Science
Department of Management and Entrepreneurship
University of Turku
Email:
Mobile:

APPENDIX 3: Acronym Table for Incentives for Healthcare Information Accessibility

Incentives for healthcare information accessibility	Acronym key-words	Acronym code
Internet resources that deliver HCI with special arrangements for VIP of a specific country.	Internet Resources	IR
Companies/Organizations that deliver HCI with special arrangements for VIP.	Organisational Support	OS
Assistive technologies put in place to help the VIP access HCI.	Assitive technology	AT
Special legislation, policies, processes, or systems put in place to satisfy the HCI needs of the VIP.	Legislation, processes and systems	LPS
Education to help VIP to get access to HCI.	Educational support for HCI accessibility	ESA
If policies, processes and systems designed take into account the different demographic conditions of the VIP.	Demographic consideration system design	DCD
Obligation to mark medicine packages with braille text.	Braille marking obligation	BMO
Economical and other support measures taken to support internet access of VIP.	Economical support for internet accessibility	EIA
Measures supporting VIP in their access to HCI.	Measures supporting accessibility	MSA

APPENDIX 4: Acronym for ICT Performance Indicators

ICT performance indicator	Acronym
ICT use and government efficiency	ICTG
Accessibility of digital content	ADC
Availability of latest technologies	ALT
Impact of ICT on access to basic services	IAS
Laws relating to ICTs	LICT
Government procurement of advanced technologies	GPAT
Quality of educational system	QES
Capacity for innovation	CI
Affordability	AF
Skills	SLS
Extent of staff training	EST
Government success in ICT promotion	GS

YOUR KNOWLEDGE HAS VALUE